First printing 2015
Printed in the United States of America
ISBN 978-0-9916543-7-6

Published by
Graphospasm Kollabrative, LLC
dba RewCrew Collaborations
Sparks, Nevada

Cover Illustration by
Turi Everett, Sweden

Layout and Design by
Double Click Design, Reno, Nevada

Printed by
Abbott's Printing, Inc.
500 S. 2nd Ave., Yakima, WA 98902

A Glimpse into the Abyss...

My first exposure to grapefruits was at my Grandparents' house in Ronkonkoma, Long Island, New York. To me, there's always been an elegance to the grapefruit, so I thought was you had to be rich to enjoy this delicacy, but average people devour them all the time. Grandma Mooney sectioned them, drizzled honey or sprinkled sugar, broiled them, and served with a cherry on top.

For years, the grapefruit has been my unconditional pal. It can be yours, too. It loves us when we're dieting or just when we want the nutritional value. Their original cluster form reminds me of family, though their unpredictable bittersweetness does, too. Life, like a grapefruit, can be bittersweet for all of us.

Sections of My Grapefruit include:
poetry, short stories, dreams, musings, astral travel, life, loss, love.

I create my work to be accessible to any reader. My creations represent a moment in time...a moment of my time which can equate to yours as well.

I'm far from a traditional poet because I love audacious forms which take shape as I write. I let the poem and/or subject choose the direction... I'm merely the veracious vehicle from which they exude. Enjoy the occasional Rant, Haiku, Ode, Acrostic, Onomatopoeia/Echoism, Pastiche (pas·teeche), Hyberbole (hy·per·bo·lee), and Aubades (ō-'bäd).

We all experience nostalgic glimmers, sentimental sparks, pulp fiction flashes and reality clusters of separating sections, peeling the rind, stinging pain, and if you are as lucky as me, the juicy joy of experiencing new landscapes.

I live truthfully through my poems. Forbidden fruit and unconditional love should be exposed and shared. I hope there is something here for you...to savor, to enjoy, to borrow!

Welcome to my world.

Sustaining my courage and speaking to me for years,
a mantra from the master, Winnie the Pooh:

*"When you are a Bear
of very Little Brain,
and you think of Things,
you find sometimes that
a Thing which seemed
very Thingish inside you
is quite different when it
gets out into the open
and has other people
looking at it!"*

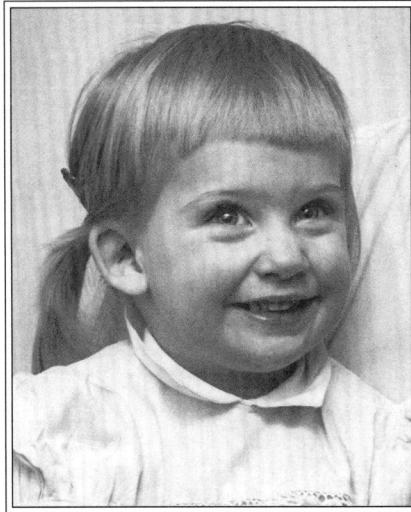

Bitter & Sweet Dedication

My husband Dale asked me one day if I ever miss my mentor, friend, poetry pal, and personal wizardess, Joyce Cannon.

I told him only...
when the sun is shining over the Spanish Springs Valley of Northern Nevada or
when I see a party of Stellar Jays in search of mischief or
a drift of Quail in pursuit of happiness or
when I am reading Phil Cousineau's *Stroking the Creative Fires* or
wrangling a Journal Juju or Dose of Mirth from *The Modern Day Muses* or
when crafting poetry...or
when I breathe.
That's the only time I think of Joyce Cannon.

Joyce Cannon graced my life one day in late 2007 at Unnamed Writers Group.

In the cafeteria of Northern Nevada Medical Center, we met for *free* coffee to get to know each other, discuss our poetry ideas, and goals for publishing.

Ironically, NNMC is where she spent many of her last days, but I felt comfort, not sorrow, knowing she and I often discussed how life brings you full circle...you'll just never know how or when.

As we sipped awful coffee that fall day, we first agreed we deserved Starbucks coffee from then on and then made a pact to be each other's cheerleader and poetry groupie.

We challenged each other with creations of veracious poetry, we gathered other creative poets, we researched and cackled about birds, we marveled at full moons, we honored our Medicine Cards, we bantered life and family, we solved world problems, and we reveled in what the universe had planned for us and how we would oblige this Big-Bang-Theory in return.

She left us too soon in early 2013 at 82 years young.

Joyce Cannon battled her own demons, but taught me well how to manipulate mine to my advantage or at least how to make deals with them to survive.

Joyce was audaciously wise and I am a much better person for it.

For the wisdom, the love, the comradery, and the hugs she shared, I dedicate this book to her, my mentor, my personal wizardess.

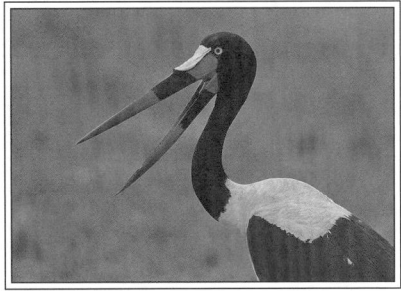

The Saddle-Billed Stork was Joyce's favorite bird.

A Tisket, A Tasket
Foster Kittens in Basket

Gently
    Sift out worry and fear
    Tenderly fold in security
    Add warm blankets and baskets
    Spread love over the babes

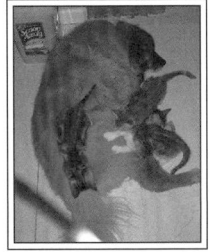

Gradually
    Mix well with daily socializing
    Alternate cuddling and nap time
    Combine kitten kisses and hugs
    Blend trust and boundaries

Compassionately
    Interchange soft and crunchy meals with water
    Scoop necessary discard
    Reinforce positive behaviors
    Smooth relations with other pets

Productively
    Nurture this bundle of joy to be pleasing to society
    Bathe, clip claws, brush...repeat
    Weigh daily for 2lb benchmark
    Deliver balls of fluff for a family to cherish!

10/29/10
This 'Recipe for Life' is in honor of Nevada Humane Society Foster Kitten Parents.
We fostered 17 from July thru September of 2010. Klondike, pictured with his monstrous
white paws on KareBear, is the only one who stayed. This poem is for all those empathetic
pet lovers who step into the dainty, yet giant shoes of a mother cat, so these abandoned
kittens have a fighting chance.

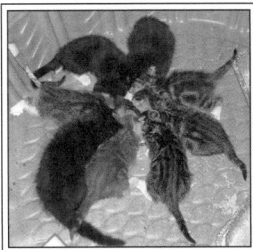

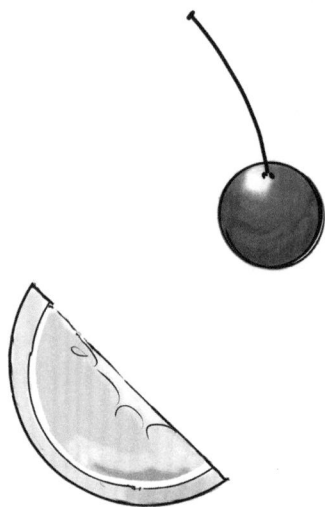

Analogy of Animalistic Authority

Akin to zebras, Referees crisscross fields of turf,
stripes against solids dart back and forth to mediate
helmeted humans of opposing herds, they tumble
in contrary directions resulting in "Touchdown!"

Donning facial omnipotence, the Ump switch-hits
his attention, hot dogs and beer are balanced on
split-fingers while dusty cleats and watchful eyes dig
in, the hippo-sized masked man roars "Strike One!"

Mimicking monkeys, arms swing and wave as
ape-sized fingers signal, gesturing to wild cheering
crowds, silver whistles Judge squeaky shoes on a sweaty
court where premeditated "Dunks are Slammed!"

2/3/01
Questioning authority

Another One Bites the Dust

Although we try to connect
in face time
in email time
in conscious time
even subconscious time,
our ever-so-busy
voracious daily yammering
much-to-do-about-nothing,
disallows
much desired
much required
much inspired
even the wildfire liaisons
humans need so desperately, but
another minute
another day
another week
even another year
quickly, yet inconspicuously
slips through our fingers
tripping us up with dubious chores,
ambitious responsibilities,
skyrocketing careers
only to elude
our calendars
our cell phones
our hearts
our need to gather
our need to connect on a spiritual level
constituting an accurate,
yet inconvenient truth
that this species does not appreciate,
but instead takes for granted the 86,400 seconds of daily-allotted animation
not realizing how
precious,
limited, but
blessed we are to have what we have,

so though a struggle it may be,
challenge yourself to cherish every moment
to inhale
to exhale
to hydrate
to rest and
acknowledge you're not ready to let your existence bite the dust!

3/14/08

Any Port in a Storm

A storm of calm, quiet,
perhaps asylum-like loneliness
is brewing, stewing,
maybe even boiling
as measurements are taken,
alterations made.

Life, as I knew it, swirls, twirls
much like a tornado
leaving, bereaving
a behavior, a zone
of comfort and familiarity
in this process of transformation.

In my harbor of intimacy
and inadequacy,
my mutated wake, my internal earthquake
is perceived or looked upon
much like wild tidal waves,
a destructive tsunami.

Weak, my spirit feverishly seeks
any port in a storm
to reform the norm,
a refuge with compassion and diversion
as I linger
in this vestibule of unknowing.

2/27/11
What is your sanctuary?

Attacked From Within

Wispy golden features highlighted fetching brown eyes
  always winking unconditionally teamed with an infectious canine smile.

The invader was well concealed, like a tick in fur,
  hard to diagnose, only time would permit its intentions and stop time.

Nurturing innards unknowingly fostered and protected the complicated,
  yet worthy adversary, Tachycardia, but she waged war.

Cheddar wedges disguised the artillery given to Kelsey,
  her blonde duster wagged wild as she ran with the wind.

Our beautiful cream-colored Lab/Golden Retriever never wavered
  in her daily routine, though the enemy fought and finally scored.

Her faculties struggled, her smile sagged from incessant panting,
  her body fatigued, her spirit weakened, but never her smiling eyes.

At Dr. Ford's office, we were greeted in the happy/sad fashion,
  relieved Rainbow Bridge had a welcoming party ready to greet our girl.

2004

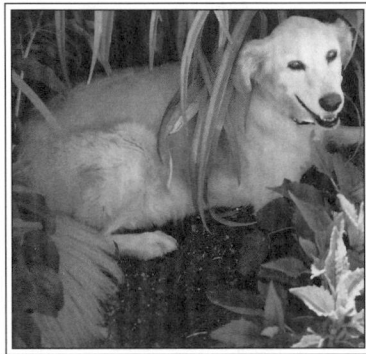

We miss you, Kelsey
1992-2003

Audacity to Stillness

Five foot five, Ma was
when a walloping stroke
forced Pa through the pearly gates.

Her health: fragile at best
Her frame: gradually weakened
Her independence: quickly diminished.

Five foot one, Ma was
when her right leg left her
in a surgical rite of passage!

Sons: she idolized all three
Sons' children: thirteen adored their Granny, Graminator, Maga
Sons' children's children: most of the nine never knew their great-matriarch.

Four foot ten, Ma was
when she surrendered obstinately
to the gateway of serenity.

Paradise: she's with Pa again
Paradise: her sharp wit is reborn
Paradise: she's five foot five again.

9/9/06
Ode to Ma. I miss ya.

Bearing the Weight of Nature

Mums bloom summer, fall
rainbow colored buds reach high,
yet bow to raindrops.

11/06

Before the Road Runs Out of Bricks

I wish to erase or maybe just soften my
painful yesterdays—
to reconstruct old bridges
scorched but not forgotten—
with appreciation for those who loved us
along
blistering
pavement
and hurtful brick-laden paths.
The desire is there to forgive their ignorance,
even more difficult to forget
a childhood barely survived—
where bruises left scars on my innocence,
my mind,
my body from
a dislocated parent in her own delayed
adolescence.
I do recall
and happily wallow in fun memories of
aunts, uncles, cousins, Carvel and Frisbee, though our
visits were so irregular.
Let's transform lost time—
Grandma's house, fireflies, the chicken coop
and come forth a reunion
of wounded, yet kindred souls,
with love and retrospect before
the road runs
out of bricks.

2/23/00
Ode to Mooney Reunions

Be Still for Now

Hush. Rest. Inhale earth.
Rehearse self-stillness before
Oomph's final exhale.

1/31/11

Bittersweet Holiday Travel

Emotions at odds
jet plane contrails mimic moods
love bears the distance.

11/10

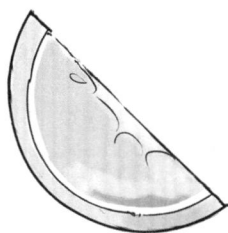

Born Without a Silver Spoon

After a Saturday afternoon of handball on Bleecker Street with friends, Frank knew time was a-wasting. He was expected at his paperboy job for *The Chat*, the newspaper of this borough of Brooklyn, NY.

It was a mild December in 1919 and as a determined young man, he always found odd jobs to help support his family. Although he was only a "newsie," he loved the newspaper business. Whether it was the hustle and bustle of watching the reporters or the smell of the ink from the noisy printing presses or just the excitement of being part of the whole system who delivered the daily news to his customers.

In a beeline to the newspaper office, he took a shortcut through the village where he was greeted by several hitched-up horses that waited with supply wagons. Patiently parked on the dusty road in front of the barber shop, the doctor's office and the town bank, the horses seemed anxious, either anticipating their masters' return or bothered by the last hurrah of fall flies. Boyishly distracted, Frank stopped and stroked each horse's mane. They appeared to appreciate the unexpected attention from the gentle teenager.

To ward off the pesky flies, the horses whipped their tails wildly. But the swishing of the long crimped strands made Frank sneeze, forcing him to grab his handkerchief from his corduroy vest pocket. Horses, he loved, but late season allergies were annoying him. Just as he passed the M.G. Babcock Land Improvement Company, he sneezed again. Looking up to wipe his nose, a windowed poster caught his eye, so he halted to read it:

"How Many Words Can You Make Out of the Word CHRISTMAS?"

Frank stared at the poster that portrayed Santa with a happy child upon his lap. He thought about the question for a very short moment and although not much of a reader, he did enjoy any kind of contest, especially one that involved words. It would be a challenge, but the prize was a silver spoon and he could give it to Mother for Christmas. Every day was a contest for a fatherless boy in Brooklyn, but this would be fun and challenging. The other challenge was the deadline was tomorrow. He'd have to hurry.

Two weeks passed. Then one evening during the dinner blessing, a knock came upon the apartment door, startling the entire Mooney dinner table. As third oldest and the eldest boy, Frank answered the door.

"Good Evening. Is Francis Joseph Mooney home?" asked a perky woman accompanied by short, squatty gentleman dressed in tweed.

"I am Frank Mooney. May I help you?"

"I am Mrs. Babcock and this is Arthur. You entered our word contest a few weeks ago. The one sponsored by the Brooklyn Eagle and M.G. Babcock Company. Do you remember?"

"Yes, ma'am, I do."

"Well, congratulations! You're our big winner!" she said with a big smile. "How old are you, Mr. Mooney? " Babcock asked. Her flamboyant hat looked as happy as she was, although her companion, Arthur stood silent. He must have been Mrs. Babcock's escort considering the Mooneys lived in a low rent district of town.

At this point, Frank's mother approached the door wondering what the fuss was all about and wanting to know what this strange woman was talking about. Frank quickly stepped in front of her so she couldn't see. He wanted the prize to be a surprise for mother.

"I am 13 and the man of this house. Why do you ask? Do I get the spoon?"

"Well..." she stammered.

Mother, a larger woman with stern eyes and a forced smile, moved closer to the door. "Won't you come in? We can chat about what kind of mischief Francis has gotten himself into this time."

Mrs. Babcock and Arthur graciously accepted and entered the tiny living room, politely removing her hovering hat and hatpin.

Again with harsh eyes, mother said, "Can you explain to me who you are and how my son is involved in the questionable contest?"

"Of course, Mrs. Mooney. Your whole family will want to hear this. Obviously, Frank is a wonderful and caring son who is very protective of his head-of-household mother and you deserve to know what this is all about."

Mother's voice softened as she said, "Oh and I admire your lovely hat. I am a hat maker in the city by trade."
Mrs. Babcock carefully set the feathered and flowered hat next to her on the sofa. "Thank you, I do love a fancy hat."

Settling in, she explained, "We are a local real estate company that sells small summer cottage-type houses and plots of land in Brooklyn and Queens. We've developed small areas of homes with fancy names like Ronkonkoma Heights and we happened to acquire a small parcel right in Lake Ronkonkoma.

Frank's sisters and brother got up from the dinner table and joined the others in the apartment's living room. Frank sat toward the forefront anxious to get his hands on that silver spoon.

"So Frank, have you told your family what the contest was all about?" she asked, extracting a large, brown envelope from her leather satchel.

"Huh, no, Mrs. Babcock, I really didn't know it if would win, so didn't want to explain it until I had to. I just love words and a good challenge, so entered the contest as soon as I saw the poster in the store window. Lucky for me, I saw it right before the entry deadline."

Besides the brown envelope, she also withdrew a slender pine box with a green velvet ribbon. In a typical teenaged sweat, Frank could hardly contain himself from jumping up and snatching it from her hand.

"Ok, young man, here's the first prize." Her eyes seemed to sparkle as she began to open the box.

Frank yelled, "NO, don't open it. I don't want Mother to see it yet. It's for Christmas!"

Everyone froze in their seats. They were startled at Frank's outburst considering he was always so polite.

"Oh, you are a sweet young man, but there is more than just this little box."

But that little box was all Frank wanted. Safely wrapped up inside was a spoon—a silver spoon. A token of a place his family only dreamed about. A place that maybe, someday, his family would get to live or at the very least, be able to dream about it each time they looked at the silver spoon.

A gift for mother was all he thought of on that late November day as he scribbled words with his whittled pencil. He had huddled in the basement of the apartment building and wrote his heart out on the only piece of paper he could find and then hand-delivered it to the Babcock office.

A very nice gift indeed, considering how poor the Mooneys were. A gift that didn't cost anything except perseverance, a little brain power and quick-thinking.

Then Mrs. Babcock broke out into laughter causing the family to giggle, too. "Frank, don't you want to show the family what you've won?"

"Yes, ma'am, I would, but I was hoping to hide it until Christmas. It's for my mother."

Mrs. Mooney reached for her son's hand and squeezed it tight. "Let's see what you have won and I will still be just as surprised on Christmas morning. Okay?"

He agreed and everyone's attention returned to Mrs. Babcock who presented Frank with the velvet box. Slowly, he opened it to reveal the shiniest silver spoon ever!

"Oh, my goodness!" squealed Mrs. Mooney in delight. "Frank, it's beautiful. How did you win this?"

Beaming, Frank was rendered speechless as the shine from the spoon practically blinded him. He was proud of his accomplishment even if mother saw the spoon before Christmas.

"Well." He started, but Mrs. Babcock interrupted him. "Here's the situation. The contest for the silver spoon with Long Island engraved on it was the first prize, but Frank also won the grand prize. Due to legalities, your dear mother will have to accept that prize for you. Mrs. Mooney, would you be ever so kind as to accept this prize for your son?"

"What is it?" Mother asked.

"Mrs. Mooney, not only did Frank win that amazing silver spoon with Long Island engraved on it, but he, or should I say you being the adult, have won a beautiful property lot on Long Island at 36 East 9th Street in Ronkonkoma!"

Silence and confusion hovered like a honey bee over a spring rose deciding whether or not to land. Frank looked at his mother, his mother looked at each sister, then back at Frank, but Frank's little brother laid on the floor playing with his toys, oblivious to the goings-on.

"So let me get this information correct. Frank won this lovely spoon and a vacant lot in Ronkonkoma. How did this happen?" Asked Mrs. Mooney.

"It's all very simple and explained in the rules of the contest, although Frank obviously was unaware of all this information. He comprised the most words out the word Christmas and now Arthur and I are here to award a wonderful young man his prizes. Due to the fact he is only 13, the prize needs to be awarded to you. Mrs. Mooney, would you accept this magnificent prize for your family on behalf of your son?"

What else could she do? She accepted the prize. The family erupted into cheers and laughter and hugs. Mrs. Babcock gathered her leather bag, her hat and exclaimed over the booming roar of Mooney voices, "Let me know when you would like to go to Long Island and see your land. I would love to take all of you for a visit."

After Mrs. Babcock left the apartment, the family just gazed at the magnificent spoon, the green velvet ribbon next to the pine box, and the envelope that accompanied them.

Then Frank jumped up and down, and then lifted his mother off the floor with a whirling hug! Frank was proud. Mother was more proud. Kitty and Martha were happy, but just sat with their arms folded across their chests as sisters do when a younger brother overachieves as Frank often did. Little brother, Daniel continued to play on the floor with his wooden toys not really caring what was happening except realizing he was hungry.

"Can we just finish dinner?" he asked. "And then talk about going to Long Island? The kids at school talk about a place called Jones Beach. Let's go swimming!"

'Far better it is to dare mighty things, to win triumphs even though checkered by failure...than to rank with the poor spirits who neither enjoy nor suffer much, because they live in the gray twilight that knows not victory nor defeat.'
—Theodore Roosevelt
(1858-1919)

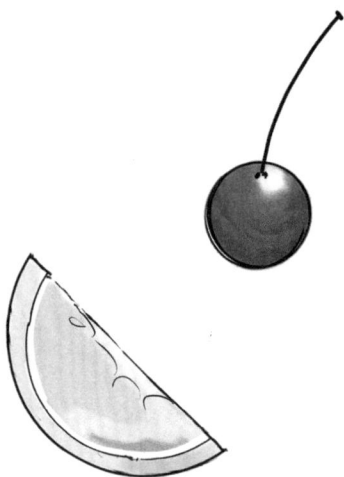

Bounty of a Stalker

Jealous tears, zealous
shadows, amplified fear roars,
frantic hearts moan, weep.

7/22/09

Brandy Reigns

Three hours, two species, one passion...
she jibs, spurs jab,
steadfast companions
embrace each other's vibes
galloping vigorously uphill against dirt and rocks
coursing a sagebrush-covered playground,
fluid as a river rushing
through the brisk desert dawn, nostrils steam
like
old
trains.

Crimped tail strands whip in rhythm
with snorts and whinnies,
eyes blink near and scan yonder,
Brandy's furry ears twitch with exhilaration
while lather gathers
and slides down
the sleek Arabian neck,
her damp brown freckles are highlighted by
the
rising
sun.

We slow the lope,
catch a breath, pull back
WHOA, dust flutters at the summit
as Washoe Valley spreads eagle below
welcoming confidants, tandem willpower
propels a wordless connection, affection, and
moist leather aromatherapy appeases the senses,
the jiggle of Brandy's tack
paces
our
thoughts.

An infrequent rendezvous
for playmates,
barnyard brats who brave
silent intellectual battles or noisy earthly storms
as they trot over tender spring terrain
and pregnant pastures...
three hours, two hearts, one passion
forever entwined by
reins
of
freedom.

10/27/99
Horses and poets should be fed, not overfed.
—Charles IX of France

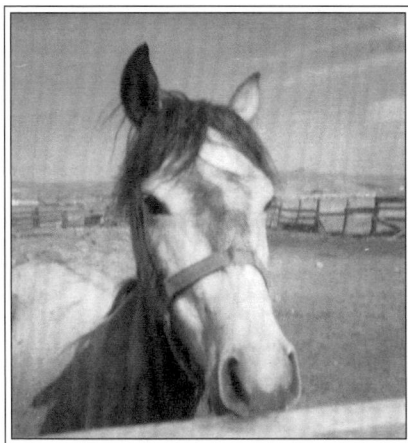

Heaven made horses from
the breath of the wind,
the beauty of the earth,
and the soul of an angel.

Captain, my Captain

Guide us not astray...
sickly, voyagers revolt,
ill pirates chart tripe.

5/19/09

Checkbooking

Spending phat in black!
Expense line swells, balance shrinks.
More so, I see less.

2/24/10
Noun as a verb

Chiming Charmer

Staggered huddled
tubes of tin, tinkle
hesitant, yet free.

Suspended by thin gossamer
strands, they vacillate
ambiguously spinning.

Whipping winds now pilot
the once pensive charm
now has chaotic thinking.

Flurries whisper
uncertainty, contemplating
tender squalls.

Now, the dangling chiming
charmer clamors, jingling
pandemonium.

Nor'easter puppets
on a chaotic mission of utter
confusion and looming love.

5/9/07

Choice

I miss something about you
but I'm not sure or don't know what it is.

Maybe it's the love-hate-love battle or
constant teamwork-rivalry that was beat into us.

I have to choose not to be with you
for you are harmful and toxic to me.

So desperate for love, we learned to take
the pain, the hate, the manipulation that came with "love."

We didn't know how to choose then,
but now I choose me, I have to choose me.

To be pain-free, bruise-free, guilt-free,
ridicule-free, to be toxin-free.

Yes, I will miss you,
but finally I love me more.

12/15/13
Giving up on something/someone.

Cloistered in '63

Inside our old Manning Hotel room, any noise scared us.
Outside, bright lights flashed through the stained hotel curtains.

We didn't know the neighbors.
We didn't know anyone in Reno for that matter.

Outside, many trains rumbled passed our downtown window.
The clickety-clack shook our bed, our toys and our little bodies.

We could hear strangers talking through the dingy walls.
We did not to open the door for anyone.

Inside our room, the old radiator rattled, clanked and steamed.
Our hearts cried when the broken sprayer soaked our tiny, silver Christmas tree.

We could hear neighbors stomping down the hall.
We huddled under the bed until Mom returned from work.

Outside, soggy sandbags were stacked like Lincoln Logs on wet sidewalks.
People dressed in black and white get on and off orange and yellow buses.

We didn't know our neighbors.
We were only three, five and seven years-old.

Outside the Manning Hotel, snow fell and church bells rang.
Inside, Terry, Patty and I, though frightened, played quietly and thrived.

11/8/06

Cold-Convoluted-Conservative-Capital

Historical brick and mortar buildings
tower over the chilled city of authority
sirens scream, cabbies honk, flags flap,
Starbucks is on every corner...
                                    ...to sooth my desires.

Fuzzy, green moss frames cobblestone
sidewalks adding color to a black overcoat
society implying indistinguishable
activity at The White House...
                                    ...in gloomy daytime darkness.

Clusters of marching umbrellas stop
at street corners as pigeons circle above,
zeroing in on the perfect target, a statue
or maybe to salute the Chief...
                                    ...in God we trust.

Vetoed branches litter the streets,
huddled, leaves and tourists gather along
the cold marble Vietnam wall, clicking
cameras depict memories...
                                    ...as warm tears freeze.

Frigid breezes blow, raindrops drift
toward the gated fortress in the heart
of our nation's nerve center, I'm not
impressed nor intimidated by its bitterness...
                                    ...I feel sorry for it.

Why am I not impressed? I try. I try.
I stare at a place capable of stealing
my breathe away, but the chill of stillness,
hidden weapons and secrets cut like a...
                                    ...knife in my back.

One last glance, still nothing – just dogs
walking people, Georgetown students
shouldering backpacks, debating lectures
and lunch in DC where any deliberation...
                              ...oddly can become historical.

3/1/09
My perception at the end of the Bush years,
but a brighter landscape was on its way.

"Poets are the unacknowledged legislators of the world."

Percy Bysshe Shelley felt poets were not only authors of language, of music, of the dance, architecture, statuary, and painting; but institutors of laws and founders of civil society as language is arbitrarily produced by the imagination of a higher beauty and truth.

In Shelley's opinion, a poet has a deep, mystic appreciation for nature and this intense connection with the natural world gives him/her access to profound cosmic truths. Poets have the power and the duty to translate these truths, through the use of imagination, but only a kind of poetry that the public can understand.

Thus, Shelly's poetry became a kind of prophecy, and through his words, he felt a poet can have the ability to change the world for the better and to bring about political, social, and spiritual change, though poets are often doomed to suffer because their visionary power isolates them from other men/women and are misunderstood by critics.

In the end, however, the poet triumphs because his/her art is immortal, outlasting the tyranny of government, religion, and society and living on to inspire new generations.

Shelley's creative works were brought to the world by his widow, Mary Shelley (author of Frankenstein) after his death (1792-1822).

In 2008, Charles E. Robinson, University of Delaware English Professor, determined Percy Bysshe Shelley co-authored the novel: "He made very significant contributions in words, themes and style. The book should now be credited to both: Mary Shelley with Percy Shelley."

Come Hell or High Water

Bronx Greyhound heads west,
Reno's bright lights shout divorce.
Sandbagged, '63.

1/21/01

Common Courtesy of Late

Whispers of thanks, none
Sneeze skips heartbeats, bless you not
Door, open thyself.

3/12/08

Cookin' with the Captain

A mentor of manners, a master of jokes, he
and Mr. Green Jeans bantered, some forty years.
Piglets, llamas, donkeys, and Bunny Rabbit
pranced and danced to children's cheers.

Now what to do, Captain Kangaroo
pondered, retired with so much free time to use.
How about a cookbook about unusual delights
to categorically satisfy, mystify and amuse.

Mister Moose Minestrone, mucho tasty,
but Dancing Bear Dumplings were also great!
However, Oven Fried Orangutan BoBo
the cast desired, begging him to orchestrate!!

Friends, fans clutched *"Cookin' with the Captain"*
from this eccentric, yet generous old gay man.
Book proceeds were donated to countless animal
groups, proving this the oddest story to understand.

7/21/09
Writer's Digest Magazine Challenge: *Take a celebrity, flip-flop
their career and take them in a new, exciting direction.*

Dance of Conception
—In honor of Nevada artists, creative beings, entrepreneurs.

Zeal and zest brainstorm,
an impetuous struggle begins
all to conceive and contrive a labor of love,
all knowing the impending
artistic process...a love affair will ensue.

Like man and beast galloping up
a sagebrush-scented hillside grappling against dust,
inner reflection materializes,
fearless inspiration leaks out into
puddles of exhausted eye water...sobs, sweat.

Juices jell, plots thicken,
colors blend as our singular disciplines
sequentially demand uninterrupted
seclusion, isolation and meditation,
full moon darkness...Nevada coyotes serenade.

Infinite moments in time disintegrate,
but ambivalence is revived by distinctive
muses: lap cats purr and twitch,
a potter's wheel spins, commissioned for duty,
discarded wrinkled paper blooms...a canvas dries.

Camaraderie of creative peers
quenches the creator's thirst like
a sinuous waterway on parched high and low
deserts, a rare but wishful whim, our cold desolate
dawn causes nostrils to steam...reminiscent of the V&T.

Willpower thrusts a rough draft
in tandem with shameless rhythms of
grumbles, mumbles, mutters, stutters,
snorts and bellyaches,
fruition comes to pass...fear and doubt be gone.

The rigorous deliverance of
a peculiar yet powerful interpretation
begins, birthed from rebellious
phantoms and tantrums, an innocent
inner vision emerges...coddle the sweet triumph.

Harnessed by reins of historical perseverance,
some mine their talent
others gamble with innovative distractions
egos embody inherent battle born dreams as
a victorious whisper is exhaled...a well-deserved climax.

Spent, the artiste' feels incredible fatigue,
as a dazed, blurry and bloodshot, though
frazzled, contentment blossoms
tears of honor, accomplishment and affection
trickle upon the delicate babe...so timid and coy.

Despite the imminent sleepless silver blue nights,
surviving grim gray critiques of scarlet pens,
embracing the rejections, though
honoring endless rehearsals, marathon rewrites
and re-dos...hot-off-the-press, curtains rise, kilns cool.

3/24/04

Deep Pile, Big Smile

A red on/off switch is sporadically activated,
self-propelled eagerness trembles, vibrates
as white noises soothe hungry acoustic organs.

Dark crevices await the variety of tools that
can manipulate individual needs, they are drawn,
partial to neglected sensations and forgotten flecks.

Sinless joy mimics erotic pleasures, giddy
guiltless sweat is fused with elbow grease
as artful impressions are left on twisted fibers.

Sprightly caress of expert hands harmoniously
hides away attachments as ambidextrous pulsation
is enjoyed, satisfying physical repetition culminates...

...ah...ah...ah...
Vacuuming

10/30/00

Dismal DMV Day

Blue cars pace green cars
in senseless lot rationale...
No parking for you!

Kids cry, phones ring, snooze
hurry up and wait, stare, sneeze...
G5, counter 10.

12/10/09
Wild Women in Paradox

Do Not Disturb

In the thickest of night, life as you know it
—can suck thanks to others.

In a fleeting moment, an exhausted existence
is haunted with doubt, the headache returns.

Your personal house of cards shifts,
your soul alters, spirit swings low.

Crowded emotional escalators intensify, up
and down, creaking and thumping.

A tipping point of thoughts zeroes in,
targeting turbulent internal deliberation.

Self-worth wobbles, causing one to wonder if
defending one's space is logical, rightful, or just selfish.

In learning to love one's self as is, technical circumnavigation
is required if inner turmoil is to be smoothed over.

Every miniscule palpitation of self-reflection bumps
and grinds, intermingling in the midst of others.

Those "others" can be in pursuit of
enabled happiness
total control freak mode
crying wolf
wanting to be rescued
adults wanting to be parented or not,

so it may be best to consider becoming a hermit
and hang up a "Do Not Disturb" sign.

12/13/10

Do Ya Remember Where We Came From?

Do ya remember where we came from,
    when did this merry-go-round all start...
do ya remember the nice house in the trees
    before our family was torn apart?

It all started for us sisters
    traveling, 35 years back...
in and out of Greyhound Bus Stations
    traveling, from east to west to be exact.

Same clothes, same Misty dolls,
    same toys, same room, same bikes...
children long to control things when
    not allowed to have individual likes.

Now adults—who think they have it all,
    sometimes forget where they began...
and have shut down the emotional connection,
    afraid to help a brother, their fellowman.

If one can not control it all or
    lend a helping hand, why bother...
unconditional love should be the key
    when it comes to our blood-brother.

Do ya remember where we came from
    good times, bad times, then and now?
We're still the same people in a different time,
    can you find it in your heart to love us somehow?

2/14/99

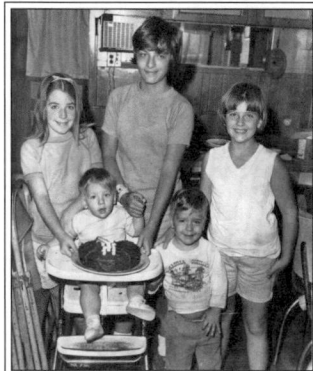

Dream-Scape Goat

Last night a goat I dreamed I was
with split hooves and fur so bristle.
Short were my horns as was my tail
what's become of me, I chew on thistle?

Me and Billy goat pranced 'round the corral
as evening brewed, we await treats and hay.
With woody teeth, we click and clack
to bully the horses, keeping them at bay.

Carrots and apples and grain we nibble
fat and sassy, our bellies grow chubby.
What else for farm pets to do, but eat
and sleep and roll in mud to get grubby!

Music, voices, in the barnyard I hear,
I'm dizzy with blinking and a rata-tat-tat.
Have I become a smelly old goat? Silly me,
it's my alarm, I am really just a barn cat!

2/13/08
"Last night I dreamed..."
Ode to Natalie Brown, a stubborn old Spanish Springs goat

Dreams to Creation

Intensity.
Obsession.
Infatuation.
Fascination.
Restless, abstract
passion of formulating,
no...crafting poetry, mining
it from the deep dark crevices
of an artist's imagination, though
occasionally, the eruption rears its argumentative
head desperately in search of veracious, tenacious yet
supreme vehicles to afford, assist and facilitate the culminating
journey that only elite, powerful and innovative Nevada Poets can achieve.

2000
This poem was published in PEGASUS *in the Winter 2000 issue.*

Era of Majestic Innocence

Drapes of red velvet,
popcorn, dark kisses, necking,
Dracula awaits.

January 2001
Dedicated the Majestic Theatre in Downtown Reno—1900s-1975
Published in Reno Gazette Journal *poetry contest in May 2001*

Evolution

Anxious,
yet strong-willed,
Joyce faced
every emotion head-on
weathering all outbursts—
Courageously aware
of vengeance
or obstinate isolation,
she triumphed with
veracity, vigor
and sparkle—
honoring her true
luminous
individuality
without compromise.

2/17/08
Happy Birthday, Wild Woman Joyce Cannon.
Love, Peg

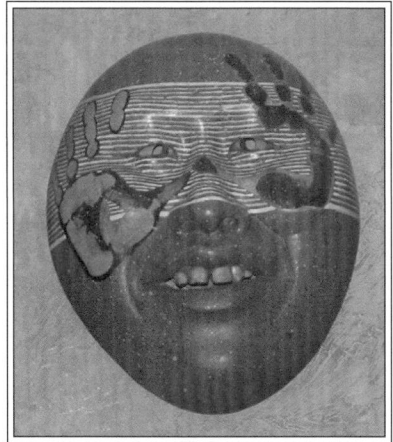

Facade of Serenity

The sun rises despite
obscurity shadows the room,
Mommy lovingly tucks my head safely beneath her chin
hugging me tightly
she yells bad words at Daddy
I cover my ears
brother hides behind the curtains at the front window
the garbage man outside waves to him
our new baby brother cries
the TV screams
and upon our cold mac and cheese, the sun sets.

2/17/09
When parents fight.

Faithful Monotony

With intrinsic
purpose, budding leaves
flutter on tender branch tips
of a sturdy Quaking Aspen colony
as aromatic, sugar-sweet blossoms
on Flowering Cherry twitter awkwardly,
yet gracefully in chilly mischievous spring squalls.

Concurrently underfoot
of grazing Jerseys and Holsteins,
tender lime-green blades of Bluegrass
and Zoysia emerge from humus-rich earth,
sprouts are skyward, in congregated clumps
spotting and dotting pastures and meadows like measles.

Mother Nature,
quite the predictable,
over-achieving Wallflower, validates
herself perennially with unwavering strength,
enchanted fingers of fragrant creativity, Chinese Lantern
illuminations cheering us, and a magical memory to Forget-me-not.

4/29/09

Flip Side of Impossible

When personal challenges arise, we assume
our chosen end result is impossible...
though gaining new perspectives...
searching out broadened landscapes...
choosing to see the journey with new eyes...
can make the outlook somewhat tolerable.

It is possible to be a caretaker-type, improve
yourself and continue being a positive role model.

It is possible to purge material belongings
without deleting treasured memories.

It is possible to make healthy nutritional choices
without sacrificing the happiness of your taste buds.

It is possible to rekindle intimate affection in slow motion,
enjoy partners, making the most of a moment in time.

With your creative talents, a satisfying future is achievable...
catch sight of your excursion with fresh eyes...
be happy in your own homey haven,
pursue excitement, if only in your dreams...
acquire new-fangled angles so as life's challenges arise,
you're ready to hang on tight and ride the waves with wild abandon!

8/3/11

From Pillar to Post, We Wander

For survival of the fittest,
Riddles banter in our hearts and minds, questioning why
Opposites attract, wondering if
Men really are from Mars.

Positive principles, thoughts and attitudes
Intoxicate our psyches, buoyant enough to
Lift any of us to limitless
Levels of confidence mirrored by
Affirmations of certainty and sincerity, a pinch of
Rhapsody is added for exhilarated flavor.

Trickery or even treachery, though, may
Occur, but lighthearted

Poetry, prose and points of view
Oppose mischievous sprites and evil distractions that attempt to
Stump our goals and ambitions, be steadfast of the optimistic
Treasures of each wanderer.

With motivated allegiance, passion and
Enthusiasm, each determined soul must

Whittle down an inventory, as unique lists of
Attributes set mortals apart, yet
Noteworthy, honest details must
Demand nothing less than more to
Energize job interviews or alien encounters. Ambiguous
Ranges of emotion support choices...stay strong, don't ever surrender!

5/19/09
Acrostic

Garage Sale Goon

She moaned, she whined
begging for kindness
as she fumbled her purse
digging for coins.

I had no mercy
as the heat beat down
she was going to pay
a dollar like everyone else.

She mumbled
begrudgingly dragging her feet
along the simmering concrete
handing over wrinkled bills.

In the end
she paid my price
took her treasures
I smiled, she drove away.

But then noticeably
something was missing
she got even with me
by stealing two other items.

The human spirit is
feisty, resilient, yet cruel
always wanting a deal
without paying full price.

7/2/08

Getting Naked

   To reveal one's
inner self
outer self
works of art
emotions
musings
shadow side
   or other precariously personal parts subtly or
   by
accident
spontaneity
intentional
cognizant
subliminal
impulse
   can result in enormous exposure which then
   triggers
risks
intimidation
expansion
depletion
evolution
promotion
   empowering artists so they can master the art
   of
dexterity
proficiency
creativeness
creepiness
imagination
craftiness
   to become more comfortable when getting naked in front of peers is a
   necessity!

11/25/11

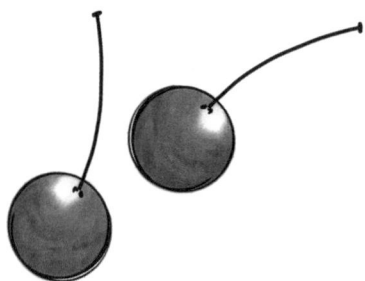

GRACE

Do we wear it?
Do we put it on our face?
Do any of us deserve it?
What is this thing called Grace?

It is a God-given virtue
presented with love.
It makes us feel so good
from whomever below or up above.

Grace, a prayer or a blessing
in many a different place.
Before a feast or a supper
A holiness we can embrace!

A divine influence to help
us all do our good deeds.
Sharing our lessons and beliefs
at a rate of God-speed!

Grace is not made of material
like burlap, fabric or lace.
Nor made of sticks or stones
or anything you can trace.

It describes our personality,
our choices, attitudes and actions.
So keep your chin up and reach
for the heavens in great Christian fashion.

Share Grace with others, reveal your
soul, don't just let your heart roam.
'Cause your strong family is keeping
the faith and leading us all home!

7/28/99

Grandma Mooney

Fingers, saggy and worn, tenderly tatted with
age dots, a thin lackluster
gold band still adorns her left hand .
Hands of rich Italian descent articulate vigorous, enchanting emotion
with persistent movement. Fingers
reach around a round, effervescent figure to tie an apron,
evident stains from
years of stew stirring and cookie conjuring.

Hands, Grandma's, wave to us through her weathered
kitchen screen door, donning gravy
whips and soup ladles like they were magic
wands. My fingers were caught in the
cookie jar on many occasions, but
this time, my matriarchal magician caught me dipping one
in the butter dish.

2/15/10
Internal acrostic

Grandpa Mooney

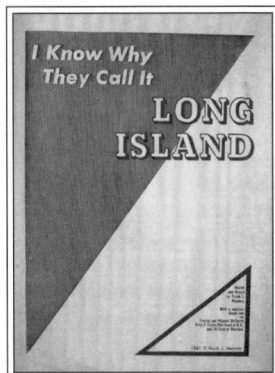

```
SCRAMBLE
 O
 N
 T
 E
 SWAYS
 T   O
     U
     N
     G
     S
   INTO        W
     E       OPENING
   ROLLERCOASTER    A
      I        D    TO   D
     OF        P  VENTURES
      E        L    S    S
               A    I    S
               Y    R    C
                    I    R
                 NIGHTFALL
                    G    B
                         B
                         L
                    GAMES
                      N
              PENCIL-DANCING
                         A
                         R
                         E
                         E
                         R!
```

(Scramble Contest sways youngster into rollercoaster life of wordplay opening gates to ventures desiring nightfall Scrabble games and pencil-dancing career!)

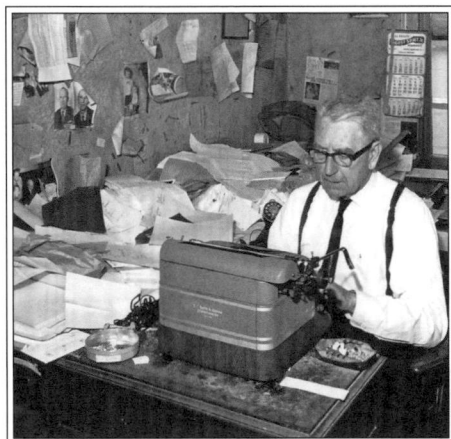

Harness Winter, Unleash Spring!

Puffing icy breath
ruthless temps halt life's sparkle
free all souls, toes, soles!

2/27/11

Hodgepodge Café of Caffeine, Comfort and Chaos

Served in cobalt-colored cups,
whipped cream topped Cappuccino
is sipped
by Boulder College coeds who
prefer their coffee bolder as
they chatter, banter truth and fiction concurrently
as clear containers of
captured coffee beans
are accidently knocked off the counter
by a waitress causing them to
crash on the concrete,
instigating ethnic diversity and
pandemonium,
multi-colored, multi-cultured beans
scurry in every direction
across the floor like cockroaches in Columbia.

5/8/00

Hotel Manning

Three New York girls snowed-in at a flop house in Reno
Steam radiates long days, mom worked at the casino.
    Scared, but safe in our fort under the bed,
    Huddled, whispering all that was said.
Darkness brings Mommy home with a new name of Keno?

6/20/07

House of Cats

Mama Dove's coo sends a Morse-coded
rhythm to yet another nest of dovelings
in the still of a sleepless summer twilight.
Their secrets, their stealthy plans, I hear.

Pigeon kin fly in and out from their new nest
clicking, clacking, tipping, tapping as if wearing
dance shoes to clatter upon my concrete tile roof.
Busy, busy, I adore their nurturing.

No hammers, saws nor building permits in tow,
the dogged, darling Starling family moves back in
ignoring bird block and barriers, just chirping, cheeping.
Detouring their return, my effort is thankless.

Evening shadows fall as our feisty, four-legged felines
locate and embrace their individual lairs to ensure beauty
sleep for another day of being the first line of defense.
My tenacious avian tenants, I ponder their brazenness.

Do our fine feathered friends even care that this estate
is safeguarded and fortified by this clever quad of
cunning cats who lie in wait for the next interloper?
Flights of fancy, I slip back into my delusional dreams.

8/13/08
Rew Crew Cats:
Kitty Smurf, Kritter, Koala, KindarKat, Kirby,
Kricket, Kooper, Kwincey, Klondike, Kokopelli

Human Butterfly Pool Party

Geared up
with water wings and pigtails,
delicate Aphrodite-like creatures
plunge
into a man-made lagoon
one
after
another.
A huffy Monarch puffs
on a Viceroy
and motions to little Ursula to swim
the butterfly stroke.
Rhythmically,
seven skimmers in yellow, pink and black
follow her lead,
gliding gracefully
across the cool pool
like smooth, shiny skippers
dipping in,
then out
on a pond deep in the woods.
Flitting and fluttering,
wild laughter echoes off
the rippling water,
as the swarm sips and slurps
strawberry smoothies
and serenely slip
into terrycloth cocoons.

6/2/04

I Found My Dad

There once was a dad
    We'll call him Art.
He had three little girls,
    One was "Peg of his heart!"
But in November of '63
    without warning or notice
The girls disappeared with their mom
    causing an emotional injustice.
He knew not where they went
    or why their mom stirred such distress.
So now his world was torn apart
    leaving him alone, feeling helpless.
A dozen years went by
    Art still suffered the void.
But he moved on with his life
    and found another family to enjoy!
Then in 1975, Uncle Mike in New York
    called Art, taking a chance.
A teenaged girl, Patty, was at his house
    could he make an appearance?
The other two girls were way out west
    Terry in college, Peggy's a wife?
The thought to reunite was unnerving at best,
    "How can I make up twelve years of my life?"
It is now 14 years later, July 1999,
    Dad came for a quick visit.
Tagging along was his longtime friend, Willa,
    A nice lady we had to admit.
But at 40 years old with a wandering mind,
    Peg of his heart was struggling.
With the thought of other people calling him Dad
    And the many families he was juggling.
There are still times I want a Dad
    of my own, not wanting to share.
I grew up fast to survive, hoping and
    praying to have parents there.
The visit stirred emotions for everyone
    especially this little woman-girl.
Even with the future iffy for all,
    when are you taking ME to Disneyworld?

7/10/99
I love you, Dad.

Job Opening with the Devil
(an equal opportunity employer)

Necessary Qualifications:

Literally Mischievous,
Naughty
Overpowering Protagonist
Quandaryless Resolution
Strident Temper
Uncertain Vapid Warrior
Xenophile
Youthful
Zeal
Appropriately Balanced Cynicism
Deported
Excruciatingly Freakish
Garish
Hectic
Incites Jealousy
Kyphosis

If you harbor these traits,
please go to directly to Hell.

6/2/09
Twisted alphabet poetry: L-K

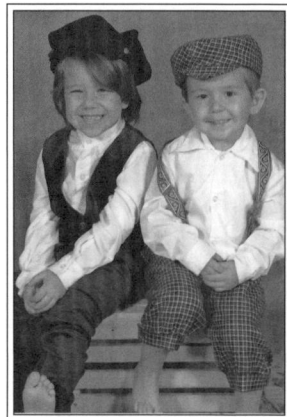

Joyride

Southern tailwinds whip
through my ratty straw hat,
sweaty uncombed tresses
dangle heavy below a ragged brim.

Downy Poplars and Cottonwoods
whistle trivial summer tunes
as relentless muggy days
slip slowly by with vivid whimsy.

Our teeth—gritty,
our hands—mudhole dirty,
our heyday adventures—simple,
Grampy's ramshackled Thomas Flyer—classic.

We slap mosquitoes as feathery grass
strands hung silly from our smiles,
I giggle at Chase, Ryder and Jaxon—
tomfoolery kids in curious cahoots.

In our convoy of make-believe,
four drivers bounce on disintegrated
red leather car seats pretending to steer,
three corroded cylinders pretend to motor.

Rusted fenders and retired axles rest
upon rotted wooden blocks while
juvenile horn-honking inspires
never-to-forget joyrides of make-believe.

8/29/04
Rev. 4/4/11

Kentucky Bottomland Ensemble

In the groins of dense secluded woods,
my senses awaken to damp shades of daylight,
stubborn and obstinate,
misty fog wafts through a brotherhood
of willful tangled tree branches
reaching, desperate to connect to one another.

A consortium of creatures,
some perverse – some cheerful,
prepare their idiosyncratic artillery
for the morning's production. Each winged
soprano and chirper claims its perch,
perfecting its remarkable predestined arrangement.

Co-conspirator to drizzling fog,
dribbling streams ration nourishment
to the wooded community. Reckless or docile,
ancient agendas merge into a rhythm
to express extraordinary yet significant contributions
to nature's moment of multiplicity.

I statue myself, roosting in a pinkish-leafed Redbud
that stands proud in this Red River Gorge
Paradise. I clutch the slick black bark as dew
slithers past my fingers to thirsty youthful greens –
bubble gum-colored buds obliquely
dangle from each tender twig tip.

The dawn hums, white noise strums
and kicks off a traditional southern ensemble
with chortles and sniggers,
a daily ritual performed in secret depths
of the wicked ecological diversity
of Kentucky's undiscovered Bottomland.

4/9/10
Ode to Eliot Porter

Kismet

Everyday Wendell, a short, gawky chap dressed neatly in earth tone colors.
Annabelle lived a few houses away, hers is lavender trimmed of pink and white.

Rose bushes of honey, crimson and blush bordered her picket-fenced courtyard.
Prickly shrubs expelled bouquets of sweetness, his allergies tickle and sneeze.

Bright in the antique Palladian window, a movement catches his eye.
He sees her white-blonde, wavy locks glisten about her smile, she blinks.

Their blue and brown eyes arrest each other, Wendell stares, almost panting.
After wintry cabin-crazy months, he may meet this elusive angel, her door is near.

Slowly, but surely the big wooden door opens, Annabelle appears like a goddess.
Cheerfully giddy, he prances on the cobblestones toward the knotty pine entry.

Wordless, they consider each other's energy and non-verbal body language.
Slowly shuffling to the plaid sofa, Wendell and Annabelle become fast friends.

Friends come, some go, lucky be you if they stay loyal and true.
Fingers, toes and paws are crossed in hopes friendship lasts forever.

2/07
Dedicated to Wendell, the Basset Hound
and Annabelle, the Golden-Doodle!

Knack Attack

As night sentry for the perimeter, I spy.
Accountability is a priority, I patrol.

Situating my sights, I scan the grounds.
Senses shudder and twitch, I detect a perp.

On target, I pounce and hold the trespasser hostage.
Outwardly, I appear vicious, yet methodically playful.

In good faith, I release and give chase.
In time, I will take my prisoner once more.

Quaking, it squeals, I hold tight for recovery.
Quivering, it squirms, I will win triumphantly.

A full moon smiles and sinks slowly into the night,
reconnaissance is complete.

As dawn breaks, the stilled interloper,
a triumphant gift is delivered to the back door.

9/20/10
For Super Dooper Kooper Rew

Ladies, Do You Dare?

The fat lady may sing at the circus,
but should never parade around in the nude.

Some gals dare to be athletically gay,
while others are just naturally fit and happy.

Women often speak up with a gregarious flare
as others muffle their outbursts with festered anxiety.

Daughters dare ask their mothers pointed
questions with hopes of answers without daggers.

Honesty sucks when you reveal family secrets to those
who don't want to believe, heredity is tested and DNA is deceitful.

We wild women dare the odds, conquering altitudes, attitudes and
exactitudes, yet physical and emotional gravity, far too often, is a heartless bitch.

10/7/08

Last Night Promises

Last night,
you were oogley-googley, in awe,
just gazing at me, giggling like lovers do.
I promise I gaze at you, too.

Last night,
you chatchattered plans for travel, the future,
celebrating promises, even made love in my glow.
I promise I looked away.

Last night,
you vowed to return tonight in my brilliance so
we alone could ponder and banter life, tell jokes, drink wine.
I promise to enjoy you.

Last night
we debated my mutagenesis as I shrink nightly ever
so slowly, morphing to halves to crescents, slivering to almost gone.
Promise to stay locked on each other.

Last night
is diminishing, you with coffee
in pajamas, me fading, you shade yourself from dawn.
I fully promise to return.

8/15/14
I love my full moon experiences. I have a unique cosmic connection.
Aubade (ō-'bäd)

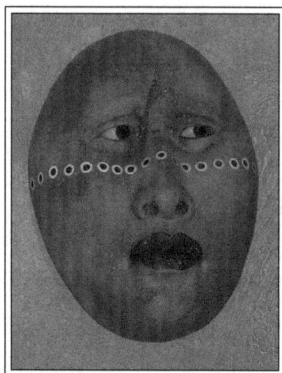

Legendary Legacy of the Notoriously Famous

Clutching their cameras
like bullfighters clutch their capes,
paparazzi often dare flustered celebrities to
charge at them in hopes of securing a
career-boosting photo opp.

Try as they may, poorly
disguised superstars attempt to dodge
screaming fans and stalkers, shunning away
for the chick click and trash flash of what will most
likely be tomorrow's scuttlebutt.

Bent and arched, the idol slides into an
intimate cafe booth, her worn Wranglers reveal
the ever so slightly, eye-catching fuchsia panty thong boasting
the presence of a rococo tattoo, resembling
a delicate dragonfly appliqué.

The hope of any privacy quickly
evaporates and the impetuous, fair-haired
goddess sniffles, a mascara tear trickles down her cheek
as she timidly slinks into the restroom to fix
her makeup and oh, tweet and text.

11/14/07
Darn celebrities and their paparazzi encounters.

Life Behind Barbs

Protected by strands of barbs,
the cool, damp meadow serenely
greets the canyon sunrise as it
reflects off all things great and metal.

Glistening with dawn dew, the galvanized
trough magnetizes scruffy creatures
with fur covered bellies bumping
like bumper cars across the countryside.

Pasture residents saunter up
to the refreshing steel destination
to quench and socialize, scraggly
tails swish in bovine harmony.

Just beyond their sturdy confines,
the valley blacksmith begins
his riveting wrought iron routine
disturbing the emergence of morn.

The farrier's clink and clank
instigates a mooing movement
of startled, sleepy calves,
heifers stumble in pursuit.

The herd shifts, the squishy
earth accepts the weight of their
decisions as mud and grass emerge
through splits of knurly hooves.

Directives are spit and sputtered,
the two-tone thunder retreats to peaceful
pastures where grazing resumes,
such is life behind barbs.

1999

Lingering Lust

His youthful gaze caressed
my silhouette, my core,
making me shudder, flutter.
I felt perfect, sexy, charmed.

    With suggestive gestures
    in hazy, starlit obscurity,
    lips kissed fingertips, skin we licked.
    I stroked his thick manly tresses.

        He dosed, I forfeited sleep
        to stare, to connect, to own
        his sense of innocence, for now.
        He wasn't mine, though I refused to let go.

            Like the torrent of a mesmerizing river,
            he forcefully followed me home
            to consciousness, a dawning moon.
            He followed, lingered, so I will keep him, for now.

9/28/09
Aubade (ō-'bäd)

Little Big Top @ Probasco & I Street

In the tranquil dressing room they shared with the
green Woody Wagon, intense trapeze artists meditate
in preparation for their afternoon performance.

Gently, they stretch pink fluorescent-striped leotards
over form-fitted, emerald green fishnet tights,
and capture their wild hair into a strict do.

From a small transistor radio, Elvis and Bobby Darin
permeate the summer air as the tiny, focused
acrobats make their grand entrance, toes pointed.

Prancing by the rowdy crowd of clapping neighbor
kids, parents, grandparents and costumed dogs,
the entranced entertainers leap into a ready position.

A shush comes over the anxious patio gathering
as they admire daring high-bar feats of precise balance
harmonized with rehearsed twirling, whirling fun.

Cheers and whistles abound for the performers,
a wonderful drifting waif of oatmeal and pinwheel
cookies signal an audacious Big Top finale.

Spellbound swing-set tumblers, Peggy and
Patty, take their bows as Terry handed out
Mom's cookies to the cheering backyard fans.

2/14/07

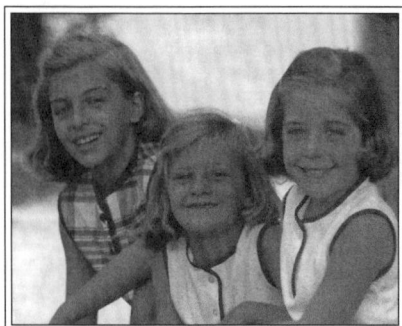

Luminous Commencement

Shadows, weightless dawn,
muted radiance, cocks crow,
blazing glow unfolds.

1/14/09
Challenge: Good Morning!

Midnight on the Black Rock

Campfire remnants swirl warm
in cool midnight breezes,
smoke signals wander
to frolic with heavy alkaline air.

Parched lips glossed with gooey,
blackened marshmallows that
leave sweet tattoos on fingers
destined to be savored 'til morn.

6/2004

My Father's Eyes

For years, I dreamed of my father's eyes and wondered
if, by wishful thinking and dreaming, I'd ever see them again.

To satisfy my longing, I wistfully replaced him with Colonel Hogan
from Hogan's Heroes, his eyes had mischief and empathy.

Hogan's similarity to my Dad's smiling eyes gave me delusions
of grandeur, apparitions for a father I would never meet again.

But luckily for me and my sisters, we did meet Dad again after
12 years and began to see the past diametrically opposed.

We discovered our father's eyes took pleasure in befuddled
disorganization, though maybe it was really creative innovation in disguise.

My eyes resemble his, some say, so I will muse over him
each time a reflection glances at me and tickles my memory.

What a sight to see: his antique tractors, car parts, tools and junk,
some say they were his best friends, his beloved family members.

No longer smiling at me, my father's eyes are smiling in celebration,
he's reunited with Grandma, Grandpa and Uncle Bob in a junk yard in the sky.

You left us too soon, Dad, but observant angels detected your
eccentric hobbies and hoped you'd fix up Heaven's old school buses.

I say goodbye for now to his memorable blue peeps, however someday,
somewhere, somehow, I will lovingly glimpse them again.

9/3/08
I love you, Dad.

My Old Grey Mares

Looking deep within the valley
of each chakra, she seeks love,
rainbows, hidden power, my crux.

Exposing my soul with her fervent mind,
a warrior heart throbs, pulses, shudders
as our minds share pure animated wisdom.

My old grey mares, yes both, love me,
gifting their sweet, earthly virtuoso-ness
with shrewd unconditional silence.

3/16/13
To Joyce and Kuzie Kue

Never Linger Long

Rolling green hills set the stage
for graduated comfort levels of seating
anticipation builds for the big show.

Beneath wispy rainbows of leaves,
speckled canine noses and pointed ears
survey the gathering as striped cats catnap.

Rust red robins and blue gray finches
take flight to enjoy the brightest of sunshine,
the freshest of buds, the best of views.

The crowd grumbles, mumbles,
my fingers gently sweep over each ivory
repeatedly like spring bees kissing sweet nectar.

Never lingering long just a rhythmic whisper,
a lullaby to my appreciative bushy-tailed
admirers, my captive audience.

Pinkie-tinkling and finger-dancing conceive
kaleidoscopic mystical melodies, a perfect
pitch pierces easy air and commands attention.

Our Maestro, with dapple paws, waves
his wand upward instigating uniqueness
to soothe every nearby savage beast.

Our juddering finale roars to a bouncy climax
inciting yips, howls, wagging, yet no applause,
my adoring groupies delight unconditionally.

4/24/11

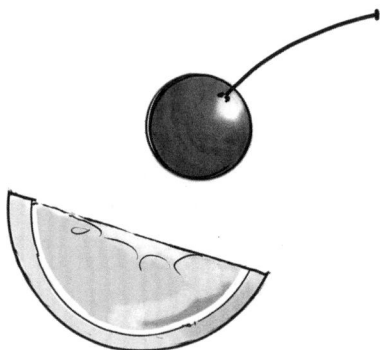

New York City's People Processor

We descend into a cold, damp passageway
where hundreds of jet-setters, military populace,
cranky baby strollers and old folks tramp
this way and that on gum-spotted concrete.

Our journey begins like the gut rumble
you get after a forbidden meal, lackadaisically
we grip filth-infested handrails, our heads bob,
bumping against graffiti-scratched windows.

The people-moving missile launches, gaining
speed, shooting recklessly through the underbelly
world of darkness as if it were spicy indigestion
passing through the intestines of the city.

Heads and stomachs turn in a death chamber
of fumes where silent, passive passengers
read their newspapers on this rolling coaster,
we look away and lock our lids to avoid nausea.

Our racing projectile sprints, then slows, dashes,
and speeds up jerking us back and forth
then stops as the monotone voice articulates
each destination and for this, we pay to exit.

3/17/09

No Carvel

"Jesus, Mary and Joseph!" was a common outburst by my mom, but this early memory was different.

Her steaming iron crashed to the hard wood floor and she ran outside. We first thought she burned herself or one us was getting into trouble.

Perched inside the big living room picture window, we watched as a wildfire of emotions engulfed our family of friends. All the neighbor ladies were screaming, "Blessed Mother, Oh My God!" They shrieked and cried, hugging each other. Confusion and hysteria took over our little street as this fateful fall day. Eventually the whole world cry for a very long time.

In Ronkonkoma on Long Island, New York, oak trees lined our dirt and gravel driveway. We stayed inside our little two-story shake-sided house silently as all the moms wept and sniveled.

Uncle Jimmy in the News Car

Just then, Grandpa Mooney raced up in his work car and we were excited. He'd often surprised us by piling all the grandkids into the big, back seat of his New York Daily

News radio news car for a sweet surprise at the Carvel Ice Cream store where we'd all get a swirly-twirly ice cream cone with Jimmie sprinkles.

This car had a big revolving golden light on top and siren if he needed it. Today the light was flashing and instead of coming into the house to see us, he leaped from the driver's seat and ran to my mom. He hugged her tight and gave each neighbor a hug, then dashed back to his car.

Terry, Peggy & Patty

Still confused, we watched Grandpa's fat blue car with the flashing yellow light speed down our gravel drive towards Hawkins Avenue leaving the sobbing ladies in a cloud of dust.

To three little girls, it was still just another day to play in laundry baskets and watch Romper Room. At seven, five and three years old, we didn't understand what the fuss was all about. I wouldn't know until I was much older, but this was the day President Kennedy was shot.

Gosh, dang it, no Carvel, no Jimmies that day.

No Ordinary Tattoo

Our Pontiac Catalina windows were tinted
grim gray from secondhand Viceroy chain
smoke, but if we coughed, complained or
even mentioned it, the worst followed.

"Obedient and congenial" were words beat
and bashed into us repeatedly as if we'd
learn from reverberation osmosis, yet
her behavior rarely assimilated them.

Splashy bath tub time disguised our
twinkling tears and let us forget our
flickering fears, using the bubbles to
wash away the discoloration of our skin.

Now we still got hugs and kisses, our hair
was forcefully pin-curled for church, so no
one should feel sorry for us, overworked
absent single mothers don't get headlines.

In the 1970s abuse never existed, so I'd
grab my kitten, close my eyes and let my
wild and zany imagination take me to
places where pain and panic disappeared.

In our make-believe forts, kids whispered
to see who had the most bruises, yet like
a darkening moon fades into thunderheads,
my black, blue and purple eventually faded.

10/24/07
Survivor

Nonsensical Road to Nowhere

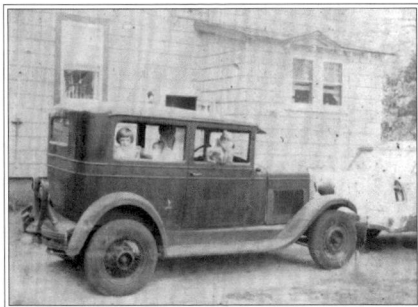

Twis brillig,
as a depleted doomsday
slithers, amalgamating onward,
horn to horn, tove to tove, bumper to bumper,
sluggishly pulsing along the impenetrable, clogged 395/I-80 artery.

> *"Breaker, breaker, Papa TaTa here!*
> *I'm modificating uh terse detouriation*
> *outta this piteous excuse for perfection,*
> *any of you circumlocutionist, sidetracking*
> *jack-knifers want to shadow along?"*

Mumbled and distorted CB gibberish forces one eye up, one ear eavesdrops,
the round rubber side begins to square, I see a tortoise pass,
the sun loiters atop the skinnying traffic
and the apocalyptic drive home
twas brillig.

3/25/09

89

Not Your Usual Tailwind

Senile as an old goat with doggie dementia,
Klementyne wandered the house, the backyard, and in
and out of the garage in search of anything or nothing.

Her 16 years were obvious as white fur shadowed
her muzzle and eyes giving her a dramatic, yet
glamourous raccoon look, and yes, she wore it well!

Outliving seven littermates, her elder gracefulness
was failing, weakening as shakiness and confusion
replaced her once energetic spirit and auditory senses.

But as nature would have it, a never doubtful, very
courteous Kirby the cat came to her rescue, as
her spotter, her guide, her tailwind.

Her satin, black fur flipped with whimsy ends
as if she had wings while his orange feline fluff
cautiously strolled next to her, as close as he could be.

Never giving the species difference a second thought,
compassionate Kirby never let Klem bump into walls
or furniture, he was the perfect escort, a guide cat.

Ignoring societal myths, Klementyne and Kirby
surpassed any assumed feline/canine ignorance
somehow communicating effortlessly until her last days.

So next time you experience an unexpected tailwind
or feel the need to be one, don't overthink it, consider
it a gift from this amazing universe of ours. Enjoy!

6/27/07
For Klementyne & Kirby

Oatmeal Mornings!

We were introduced by a friend
and became friends at a glance.
You needed me, I needed you,
so we thought we'd take a chance.

It didn't take long to discover
how much we were alike.
We shared families and lives,
an instant closeness we did strike.

Breakfast, lunch or even dinner
we broke bread and laughed at any hour.
Read our horoscopes, clean the house,
then I'd throw you in the shower.

You joked about your body scars
and for each you had a story.
But to me they showed a "tough old bird"
who lived life in all its dignity and glory.

My visits were short and sweet
but chased away the lonely days.
However, just our smiles filled a void
for both of us, in oh so many ways.

Ethel, I will miss you and our oatmeal
mornings more than anyone will ever know.
Sarcastic friends, the way you said,
"I love ya, Peg" and your hair of snow.

The Angels have taken you away,
so it's time to give their routine a try.
I'll keep memories of me and you close
but will never say good-bye.

I'm rambling on, I know you have to go,
don't let mushy me slow you down.
'Cause at the pearly gates, Walt awaits
to welcome his Girl about town.

7/21/98
I love ya, Ethel.

October Backyard Bliss

The weather shift signals all creatures,
  great and small, to hunt, gather and
    prepare to hibernate. In a hibernation box
      of winter clothes, you discover an old
        sweatshirt and pull it over your head.

Basking in the glory of this backyard, the old gray tool
  shed wonders how he and the tinkling wind chimes
    got so lucky to live here. Chirping birds send a message to
      'fill the seed feeders' and then a warm, cool, inquisitive
        breeze sneaks through the yard, a seasonal warning.

Water trickles down through ivy-draped
  river rocks as stones coax ripples across
    the pond where Poplars pop-up wherever
      they damn-well please alongside Sumacs drooping
        over the fluffy algae scarf protecting the little lagoon.

Slimy, solid gold swimmers rush to the edge excited
  about food only to see leaves with hints of fall colors fall
    aimlessly into the water. Black dogs, wet noses to the heavens,
      bark at the neighborhood while romping on landscape bark
        and mismatched stepstones under Burning Bushes.

Spent, yet still fluttering Trumpet vines dangle
  from stick and iron arbors while foot-long greenish-tan seed
    pods hang on for dear life. In their raised beds, green cherry
      tomatoes struggle to ripen in the luke-warm temperatures
        as mums of burgundy, butter and rust show off.

Green pumpkins blossom into orange trophies
  abutting weathered, fence boards that huddle around
    this peaceful compound, aged logs jointly hem each
      tree trunk in the midst of random spot gardens
        that are surrounded by "Mutt-n-Jeff" sized-rocks.

Solemnly, empty clay pots reminisce about their summer
  bloomers, but sit quietly enjoying the boredom. Butterfly
    Bushes wave goodbye, Quince Apple trees drop the last
      of their bitter fruit and Honey Locusts let each tiny
        leaf skydive, one by one.

Relaxed, you hike up your sleeves
   or maybe you could just give up on
      that recently unearthed sweatshirt altogether
         and crawl into the depths of this backyard bliss
            where Woods' wonderland actually exists year-round.

10/9/07
Dedicated to Sharon, Loki & Sassy Wood

"I always try to write on the principle of the iceberg. There is seven-eighths of it underwater for every part that shows."

– Ernest Hemingway (1899–1961) from a 1958 interview in The Paris Review.

Ol' Peg

There was a feisty lumbar disk in ol' Peg
sharing grief in her spine and right leg
the doc yanked it out
the O.R. gave a shout!
Then they celebrated over a keg!

6/27/07

Once Brilliant With Color

Glittering, ruby red lipstick glazed full, perky
lips like icy snow on a dull, brisk
winter night, even trees grieve the bitter chill.

Glitzy parties with flashy movers
and shakers are all the rage,
but this party is over, untimely some say.

The laughter and fun have ceased, bereaved
crowd thins, however confusion
and hysteria thicken, memories will be everlasting.

Suspended in muted animation, she sees dancing
and hugging continue in silence,
yet the music, the noise has been suppressed.

A sterile gathering is now set in motion
with bright lights, spotlessly clean,
the party favors are shiny and silence is steel gray.

A wet, colorless cloth wipes away the lipstick,
the audacious clothing
is gently removed, as if not to wake her.

Mortifying disbelief bites the next-of-kin
during the identification process,
then comes humiliation, reality and swollen eyes.

Now the once vibrant 'brilliant with color' mortal
lies stiff, a gray aura shadows hands lifeless
by her hips, her platinum blonde hair lacks luster.

In a tranquil pine box, she lies pale and powdered,
dressed in pasty pastels,
the pearl gray earrings involuntarily shimmer.

Humans conceive they will live forever, but the grim
reaper and insurance companies
are well acquainted with the cold, hard truth.

Business as usual for examiners in faded green
scrubs, scraping brownish crud
from underneath fingernails equals job security.

1/30/08
Crime show junkie

On Duty

Cheerfully, uniformed silhouettes deliver
flower bouquets, plants, balloons and cards—
rainbows, aromas of material love...matter no more.

Dubiously, she blinks a tear and snuggles
close to my cold steel side rails—
day by day, lonely and feeble...her misery worsens.

Routinely, our stark, colorless
blankets and linens are gently changed—
she knows not the difference...only daylight, darkness.

Valiantly, I cradle the wisdom of her years
comforting a frail, tired, tiny frame—
she clutches the call button...for security, affection.

Expressionlessly, the grayish whites of her eyes
close against me and our pillows—
she whispers shallow and raspy...faint whimpers echo.

Woefully, the hospice minister shuffles out
of our room embracing his bible—
his job is complete, he won't be back...she has departed.

Sanitarily, me and my room are decontaminated
sterilized sheets are applied, death is implied—
cards, balloons, flowers...tossed, incinerated, forgotten.

Loyally, my wheels are locked
I stand alone, on duty in silence—
waiting stoically for another patient to visit...destined to expire.

2004
Rev. 3/31/10

On Guard

Large, square and arrogant,
the steel armored beast lingers
at a stop sign, rumbling, a silent
roar of thunder is understood.

Responsibility, no matter the cost,
is gospel to the truck's defiant occupants
in a world where wickedness preys upon
treasures armored for imperative journeys.

With the speed of molasses, the composed
driver maneuvers into an isolated yard
that is bordered by discrete strands
of barbed wire and lackluster chain link.

Rattling yet stoic, a charged automatic
gate creeps back across the pavement
to its fencepost counterpart certain
all is safe, sound and secure for now.

Sun sets, trustworthy hand guns are
handed over, surrendered vests and badges
rest, another day ends without incident,
devoid of sinister activity, a job safely done.

1/7/09
Written for Underdogs of all kinds and Armored Truck Employees.

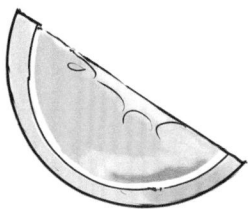

Only in MY Dreams....

Sitting on a tall, ornate chair
at a very short table,
I spy an odd shaped snow mound
in the backyard from which
a baby elephant emerges,
just as the garden ants,
saddled with their red and white
checkered knapsacks,
embark upon their journey over
sand and rocks all the while
I'm hungry, so I order food I love,
but am served food I do not
recognize in a fancy house I
have never been in with five
sets of hardwood stairs leading
to the living room surrounded by windows
that greet hot air balloons
taking flight, so I sit and
stare when suddenly
a silver hunk of a knight
scoops me up in metal arms
places me atop a white spirited steed,
blows a kiss to me
and smacks the horse on its ass
catapulting me and my feline
co-pilot into yet another
unique nano-second dream.

9/6/07
DREAMS

Oversized

In 1967, me, Dad and Mom, two sisters
and a baby brother piled into the car for
an exciting road trip, leaving the limits of Sparks
to visit relatives we hadn't seen since 1963.

Into Dad's 1955 Cadillac with white vinyl seats,
our oversized family squeezed.

What fun we would have, Daddy's Caddy's
shiny green curves and silver fenders
glistened in the heat of June as we began
our journey across the Great Salt Flats.

An oversized, but trusty burlap bag
dangled from the radiator.

The rose-colored plan included maps
to drive across our beautiful country
all the way to Long Island for our
annual New Yorker family reunion.

Corn Flakes and peaches strapped to the
car roof atop oversized suitcases.

The bright, white hard top protected us,
but couldn't dissuade the sweltering
heat even with the windows down,
the car jerked, clunked, spit and sputtered.

The oversized load of flakes and fruit was
for meals to save money.

Crankiness and exhaustion set in quickly
as our voyage came to an abrupt halt
on the salted flats as a sweaty family waited
impatiently for the dawdling tow truck.

Backing up, a timid driver stared at
the awaiting, oversized human load.

Slowly slipping within the city limits,
the driver slowed at a motel driveway
freeing himself from the exhausted,
clammy, crying crowd from Nevada.

Liberated, the tow truck rambled off
with his oversized load, steaming.

Mommy, Daddy, Terry, Patty and me
dragged suitcases and boxes to
our amazing air conditioned room,
though 4-month-old Ricky screamed!

Dismayed, the baby's petulance was due to
the oversized diaper and rash.

Amazingly, our irritability and
fatigue disappeared when we caught
sight of the big, blue swimming pool
with a matching slippery slide.

The oversized laughter in the cool water
soothed our souls and our soles.

Us kids splashed for hours with other kids
as mom and dad settled into our tiny
room while discussing dinner, but please,
God, not Corn Flakes and peaches again!

4/16/08

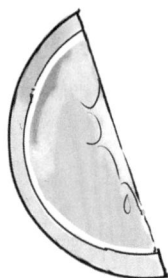

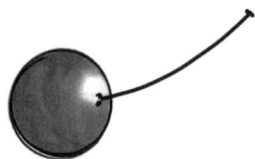

Peaceful Denial

We came looking for you
    through the halls we did walk,
following your laughter,
    hearing you talk.

But when we arrived
    our imaginations were just yearning,
for you took your walking stick
    and had begun your journey.

To a place, quite peaceful,
    Grandma & Grandpa have long waited.
Sunshine, NBA games, Reckless,
    Louis L'Amour books and gated.

We know church and religion
    were not a norm in your life.
But your faith was as strong
    as the love for your wife.

You gave us all roots
    and then helped them grow,
when we sprouted our wings
    proudly, you watched us all go.

We now walk alone but
    know you're by our side,
pondering the lessons you taught us
    as we take them in stride.

We'll keep our promise
    to take care of Ma.
So go on, rest,
    your job is done, Pa!

4/21/98
I love you, Pa

Perforation Log
Reno, NV

4/6/99 - 1045 hours:
The control room intercom blares the final warning for the
Perforation Mission. All tools and instruments, necessary
for a successful mission, were sterilized and inventoried,
checked and tested.

The chosen transport vessel has been given an expert
examination to detect any mechanical weaknesses in
hopes that it is in excellent working condition to be able to
perform this extremely important mission. All recruits have
been outfitted with proper protection gear and briefed on
the mission.

4/6/99 -1130 hours:
The exploration team assembles in the tower. They watch,
in anticipation, as the decontamination crew sterilizes the
entrance of the work area. All systems are a go.

4/6/99 -1145 hours:
The time has come. Transport begins. The route is short,
but accurate. The crew is prepared for mission commence-
ment. All necessary medical controls are switched to activa-
tion, subject is positioned, and 'away we go,' is the final
command.

1200 hours:
The interior passage, outlined in the initial blueprint, ap-
pears transparent and flimsy. The canals and cavities we are
traveling through are severely narrow with incredible detail,
but seem somewhat unstable. The explorers report they are
approaching the designated area and the ulcerated dam-
age expanse is more wide spread than originally detected.
The technical team arranges tools and instruments for easy,
yet precise access. The perforation mission begins.

1255 hours:
The goal of this team is to excavate and remove damaged
material from the designated area. This team is known for

steady hands and previous knowledge of this kind of decay. They will then spray the area with new Goldline genasal. This sterile, antiseptic application should assist the team in keeping what is left of the healthy area in tact while the work is being performed.

1315 hours:
The next step will be to bring in new material from a nearby-investigated source and attach it to cultivated area. The team will then graft the edges in hopes to reconstruct what has been left from this bizarre disaster. The end result should be that new growth progresses in the damaged area within two weeks. Luckily for this taskforce, a knowledge-able, world-renowned specialist has been drafted to over-see the fertilization and stimulation of the area so reoccur-rence of deterioration can be avoided. This undertaking is of grave importance and will be part of a science phenom-enon since recorded documentation of this procedure does not exist until now. We can only hope we can prove it will succeed. The expert who heads the exploration will be a national hero if all goes well.

1334 hours:
All systems are a go. The team will now begin closure of the graft. Protective components have been strategically placed to keep all new material from shifting. The leakage of any vital fluid is held in place during the initial healing process. Large synthetic shelters have been assembled around the area to protect from meteorological changes, seasonal distractions and airborne irritants.

Protection covering of the area will stay in place for a mini-mum of eight days. Then a removal team will assemble to discard of the covering without adverse effects to the area.

All tools, instruments and excess material, new or dam-aged, are properly sealed for sterilization and/or disposal purposes. This is vital to be in compliance with the outlines of this mission.

1347 hours:
The team retreats to the transport vessel and the perfora-tion mission is declared complete. All mission personnel

are debriefed on the outcome of the mission while equip-
ment is decontaminated and sterilized.

1402 hours:
All involved are congratulated on their stellar performances
and now return to current duties and now we await the
biopsy results.

Congratulations. You have just taken a journey to the center
of the olfactory for correction surgery of an ulcerated hu-
man septum!

June 1999
Revised April 2015

Phase of Conclusion

"I'm old, you know,
eighty-five and frail as a toothpick.

Nurse supervisor, I was
for fifty-five years in way back old Vegas
when I was perky and fun
and caring for others like you do,
but now I'm puny and tired
just waiting to die.

Nineteen-fourteen goodness, gee whiz
I'm old—can you tell I'm eighty-five?

Don't look at me,
let me look at you.
You're so pretty.
I used to be, but now I'm just old,
an old bed patient
just waiting to die.

I think I will just lay down now 'cause I'm old,
Eighty-five, I am, can you tell? That's sweet of you.

Used to be thirteen of us
but now only me and Sis and I'm two years
older but she's much sicker
and in a home but not me—Never!
Me? I'm just waiting to die."

4/28/00
(Gertha 1914-2007)

Pontrelli Piecrust

Dawn...blend, roll, caress
staunch passion, graceful crimping,
artful dough, crust...dusk.

7/8/09
For my friend, Jeany

Pulling
Heaven
Down

Dusk pulls evening to darkness as
July's full moon ascends, however,
it lingers for a spell dangling on edges
of wispy clouds and mountain cusps.

Rising as in its job descript, the lunar glow
marvels at the merriment below as captivated
crowds cheer and awe to welcome the calculated
premeditated, cyclic phenomenon.

'Round and 'round in a celebratory fashion,
rubber-soled runners, giggling strollers
and a mishmash of sandal-footed folks orbit
the concrete path of the glossy Sparks marina.

No waxing or waning, just a euphoric,
astrophysical occurrence as lazy ripples slosh
into weathered docks and tiny waves slide
slickly upon darkened beach sand reflecting bliss.

A deliberate yet serene monthly act of nature,
a free stellar, cosmological happening as
humans marvel, wonder, dream and muse in
this opportune moment of pulling
                            Heaven
                                down.

7/2/07
Full moon at the Marina

Pure Gangsta

With a sleek suspicious body style, onlookers
sense sinister activity with the vicious waylay
and dangerous silence of the Corsair.

A slit of a gangster-type windshield
conceals squinty eyes of the menacing,
elapsed, closeted skeletons of yesteryear.

Corrupt, until-proven-otherwise, occupants
loiter, the motor idles ghostly quiet in
anticipation of the impending ambush.

Thick whitewall radials begin to roll,
sluggishly inching toward the repository
into view of the unsuspecting patsy.

The full metal armor skulks onward,
rain drizzles as the driver yanks the
monetary stash from its leather keeper.

Scared, the pigeon sees it lurch forward,
only a sliding glass opening protects
him from panic of the ominous black coupe.

Slowly, the car window is rolled down,
though, only low enough to grab the
goods in exchange for cash, done!

Tires squeal out of the drive-thru across
double yellow puddles as the villains swerve
down a darkened alley near a misty marina.

Foghorns blare, sirens scream, waves swell
and whitecaps crossfire as the Phantom's thugs
huddle inside to indulge in the first of many...

...In & Out Burgers!

9/27/04

This poem was dedicated to the 1938 Phantom Corsair when it won "Best in Class" at the Cartier "Style et Lux" during the Goodwood Festival of Speed in England. An early version of my poem appeared in the National Automobile Museum's Precious Metal *Magazine in December 2006.*

In & Out Burger finally came to town in 2004!

Quarky Collaboration

Flapping individually, yet as one, they drift toward
a common goal, existence may be questionable,
but their souls harmonious, friendship contrary.

The clammy fog echoes the journeyers' forlorn
breath, sashaying lightly in search of their illusive,
water-logged comrade, hide-n-seek ensues.

Shrill hoots and hums resonate faraway,
triggering stagnant murmurs on the dreary
aquatic bath as velvet waves ripple a smirk.

Idiosyncratically, they holler, squawk, listen, only
to hear distant laughter as the wispy swish of an
expired leaf glides to a sea landing like no other.

4/14/15
Quarks were introduced to me by Todd Borg in his book, Tahoe Silence.

*This poem was inspired by a wacky, yet thought-provoking photo
of an elephant in a row boat being pulled across the waves of a
cloudy ocean by a flock of sea gulls: TEAMWORK!
Thanks, Jill Badonsky, for the image.*

Questioning Cars

Where are they all going?
An entourage of multi-colored,
metallic ping-pong balls
dart back and forth
right and left
north then east.

Is there a destination, an end game?
The naked eye
then notices several
same color cars
end up in the same
lane of traffic.

Is there a plan?
They follow each other
like Billy goats,
herded by horns honking,
fingers flipping,
thanks, but I think I'll walk.

8/23/07

Reflections, Revelations & Ruminations

Mirror, mirror,
thank you
for highlighting
well-earned representations of life,
my facial lines, creases, smile dimples and
wrinkles, the very roadmap of purposeful adventures,
victorious challenges,
involuntary tears of separateness and cheerfulness.

Mirror, mirror,
thank you
for providing
me a clear vision of who I am,
where I came from, where I'm going,
my endurance, longevity, relationships,
career goals,
the long and short of haircuts and color choices.

Mirror, mirror,
thank you
for keeping
me in check, prompting me
at naptime, giving me the ability to trigger
a variety memories and less-regretted transgressions
clearly I see
our family tree blossoming and keep hindsight of my hind end.

2/17/10

Progress
not
Perfection

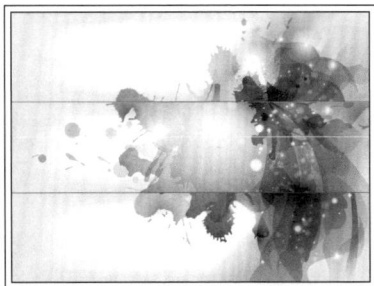

Resilience of Resident Cloud Shadows

Mystified we lurk, hovering through murky days searching for our friend,
though oddly, she's not looking for us.

> What has changed?
> Want or need us, she doesn't.

Heavy, we linger low and slow, drifting amidst winter's wind,
but somehow, feel odd shadows are cast back upon us.

> Why doesn't she hibernate?
> Climb into bed and cover her head, she hasn't.

Winters past, she sought comfort and refuge among us,
though this year, gloom has been transformed, clarified.

> What are we to do?
> This is our job, we need her, she completes us.

Januarys and Februarys of old, we've been her consummate comrade,
but this winter, we've been furloughed.

> Be well, our friend.
> You know where to find us if you ever need us.

2/8/11

Rising to the Occasion

Buoyant envelopes
wicker cockpits rise with cheers
champagne ovation.

9/3/09
Great Reno Balloon Races

Road Trip Rhapsody

The flapping straps slap
the plastic-wrapped childhood Steinway,
keeping time with the rattling trailer and whistling wind wings
as we all rumbled down the darkening mountainous highway
where we were most unfamiliar.

Stagnant radio static forced our fingers
and thumbs to thrum
the truck's aged interior, the old Ford idled rough at a late
night detour, but was willing to thunder onward and upward
to the isolated cabin for a much anticipated delivery.

Cocks crow, a dusty driveway awakens
with a crooked sunrise, the old Ford departs sluggishly,
chugging by nomadic cows hollering an impromptu daybreak wake-up call
as the rhythm of the trailer's jingling hitch chain closely mimics
a tinkling ivory love song of the love he left behind.

9/30/09
Aubade to me and the piano
(ō-bäd')

Romantic Round Table Blast from the Past to the Present

Once upon a time
    more than two decades ago,
A new pizza place came to Sparks
    and I wanted to be part of the show.

When I first arrived at the restaurant,
    it looked like something knightly.
Modeled after Arthurian legends,
    shields & swords held the walls tightly.

Sir Lancelot and the other knights
    slayed dragons and had them in tow.
But please remember, when you make
    their pizza *"no GPO!!"*

This establishment attracted many
    from the get-go, it was a hit.
Little Leagues, birthday parties, Friday nights,
    the busiest, the crew had to admit!

For the regulars, the fun never ended,
    patrons fed the jukebox with their quarters.
There were times, though, we weren't sure
    the ovens would fit any more orders.

Customers would look at the menu,
    just stand there and scan.
The pizza choices were endless and
    the crust, original or pan?

With pizza names like Guinevere's
    Delight and King Arthur's Supreme.
"Would you like shrimp and anchovies?"
    "More decisions?" they would scream!

Any true pizza lover will consume
    any given topping com-bo.
But the major determination of their visit
    was: "is this for here or to-go?"

Memories of RT have a special
   place in my life since 1975.
Salads in bowls, bartender Jack and
   teenage crews who managed to survive.

The *"last honest pizza"* is
   the way you now advertise.
Any reason, the customer is not happy,
   you'll gladly compromise.

Round Table, you should be proud
   of a job very well done.
You competed with Straw Hat for years
   and now there are none.

April 1999

Royal Pain

Scaling the silver slip-resistant steps, I reach
the tall, sun-heated kingdom above all.

Below, my subjects applaud my rise hoping
someday they, too, will achieve great heights.

All cannot attain the popular slide show, it requires
skillful talent and permission to ascend and descend.

I take a bow and perch on my aluminum throne,
peasants wave, blow kisses, throw flowers, cheer.

Baited breath, they witness slick technique, adjusting
my shorts, I conquer the smooth slide—justice for all!

Bullies exist anywhere, but why the playground? Usually it serves
as a place of power for a kid who may be powerless elsewhere.

Paybacks are hell, so we can only hope someday
summer's blistering slickness burns someone's butt!

9/30/09

Tibetan yaks from theyakranch.com, Elbert, CO

Run For the Hills

"Run"—
an invigorating premise when good
deeds go bad, energy suckers take-yet
never-give-back, forcing thoughts that
there's gotta be a better place than here and now.

"Run for"—
echoed as shadows darted, scurrying,
overwhelmed by forests of emotion where
attitudinal, spiritual vampires lay in wait to
rip out strands of hair and strings of heart.

"Run for the"—
ricochets down alleys of good intentions,
trembles across babbling behaviors, screams
over needy dead wood, ungrateful bullies,
laying in methodical waters, flopping like fish.

"Run for the hills"—
pounded in her ears, hammered inside her
heart and outside her chest, her pulse pulsated,
racing, dashing, sprinting breathlessly
to get away, as if she was being timed.

"Run for the hills NOW"—
our mere existence depends on swift
self-care and accountability and just maybe,
we are being timed as the inevitable 'game over'
will occur and slam dunk us at any time...now, run!

4/18/10

Running from the Red

Fear incessantly rushes through crimson
veins pumping a sad, carmine
heart into my throat as a rag-top cherry
T-Bird races through stop
signs of a contradictive
Catholic childhood.

Scraped elbows on redwood
divided lives—causing skinned knees, bloody
as wild minds wander back, sweet maraschinos
submerged in Shirley Temples, sunburn
making cheeks of rose
in our backyard of thorns.

Whispering, garnet
oak leaves shadowed jealousy—scarlet
anger of divorce, but daydreams of ruby
slippers pacified kids, any cheap burgundy
soothed the parental demon
until morning sky red.

Crossing against the vermillion
hand often triggered tormented
nightmares, curdling screams,
even teachers ignored obvious youthful secrets
veracity stung
as did the bruises.

Tenaciously, I twirl my strawberry
curls, another flashback, I sip my Coke
and stare: a black or blue
pen to wrangle this negative
balance in my checkbook.
I blush.

2003
This poem appeared on page one of the national poetry magazine, MOBIUS, *Sept. 2006,*
and in Western Nevada College's Wildcat Review, *Winter 2013.*

Sabbatical for a Passionate Balladist

On a purple-winged turtle, a rainbow dotted
scarf about his neck, words flutter through
billows of cotton candy clouds climbing
high on autobahns of clamoring brainstorms.

Out of the vapors, summer's last creamsicle-orange
sunset ponders its final intentions of the day
teetering upon the earth's edge with a horizon
mimicking a luscious layer of chocolate pudding.

As our lyricless voyage resumes, we bank
along magic carpets of swiggly pink and green
contrails, welcoming dusk's twinkling stars,
bypassing a gaggle of giggling grey gooses.

Smiling moon leisurely begins its rise, reflected
perfectly in an unspoiled mountain lake below,
mirroring our journey, we catch a glimpse of our
antics, grinning at the thought of this...a vacation?

Helping themselves to a sip and slurp, docile
deer and unassuming antelope sway their antlers
in unison as if to encourage the flying turtle
and me to enjoy our much needed meditation.

The sky darkens, a signal to bring closure to
this never-wanting-to-end escapade of creative
and audacious mischief that my hard-shelled,
purple-winged friend was so kind to contrive.

Now home sweet home, consonants coagulate,
letters alliterate and words are wed
to create romantic rhymes of rant and rave,
making shadows dance a ditty til dawn.

10/8/08

S.A.D.
aka Seasonal Affective Disorder

Thunderheads roll in
—like sandy waves upon the beach—
bullying nature's illuminating beacon,
light and dark airy billows wrestle
streaks of light, reluctant to finish their shift.

Winds bluster in
—like an abusive, inebriated mother—
bullying patio umbrellas and wild seed socks,
light and dark canvas and feathers succumb
to the warrior love of a summer storm.

Clouds tumble in
—like sweaty football players—
bullying independence and straightforwardness
light and dark hostility antagonizes
a fragile psyche, irritable with brittle pain.

Pillows overshadow me
—like marshmallows smothering hot cocoa—
bullying my spirit, my breathing,
light and dark blankets of pessimism fade to black,
helplessness and gloom depress my polka-dotted bed sheets.

7/28/09

Safeness of Make Believe

Recently rediscovered ancient
parts of me were found to be
not so much ancient,
but cautiously sensitive
and youthfully innocent
yearning to go back in time
to play when life was simple and fun.

Like a dilapidated barn door,
my memory hangs in gladness
of make believe and playful pretend
where accountability is only required
in mud pie making,
firefly catching
and rusty wagon pulling.

Swiftly, my memory backhands
dirty blonde bangs from blue eyes,
my barking dogs,
Scout & Parky make a delightful mad dash
just to lick a dirty face,
proving their unconditional love,
we play house.

Antiquated backyard woods sway,
September leaves scatter across the dusty driveway
where make believe and imagination
meet, so Scout can be schooled
in doll diapering and Parky
can indulge in the enjoyment
of dog biscuits and homemade dirt dinners.

10/10/10

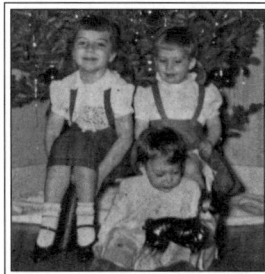

Seal Beach

Sitting on the reddish beach sand, I
wonder if and what ocean life thinks
when humans stare aimlessly out at the sea.

    Chilly waves gush over my unsteady feet,
    delivering seaweed and vacant sea shells,
    tumbling and toppling with the salty undertow.

        Marine ecospheres never dare to go near the beachy
        doorstep knowing nauseated tourists will entertain
        as they leave their boats, chum excites the sea creatures.

        So I sit, jamming my toes into sea sand, wanting
        not to return to the high, dry desert, but my watch beeps,
        my boarding pass pokes me in the pocket, urging otherwise.

9/23/09

Seduction of a Curious Nature

I wonder if there's really a man or maybe a cat
in the bright, white moon that beckons me.
I will seek him out.

I hear the grass is always greener,
the bugs bigger over the back fence.
I must investigate.

I crave to touch at tweeting birds
who heckle me at the window.
I instinctively chatter back.

My wild instinctive imagination longs
for impossible adventures, fresh air.
I follow the impulse.

My internal tomcat convinces me
to trust the hypnotic, outdoor sirens.
I am invincible.

Whiskers twitch, curiosity teases,
taunts me, I slither into a stoic trance.
Consequently, we'll all suffer.

Created by my staff, my owners,
boundaries are most critical and cloistering.
I plot to disregard them.

My spirit indulges in curious desires,
indifferent that a predator may be in wait.
I slink out an unattended egress anyway.

Curious seduction may harm me,
taking me away from everything safe and sound,
Meow, I stealthily escape.

8/14/07
Kirby & Kricket

She WAR Green Velvet!

After all was said and done,
the red tools of Christmas rested
and his green velvet heaven was a priority.

He took to the green
every snowless day, night and weekend like
sky-bound reindeer took flight on a chilly December eve.

Armed with elfin caddies, mittened
bogeys, hooded handicaps and chip shots,
Santa ventured over northern-most hills and dales.

Through green velvet forests,
he set his sights and tees, eyeballing
each anticipated fairway with a wooly-gloved wooded hand.

Hushed spectators waited patiently
to cheer, yet excited ears and tingling tails
twitched, their favorite player looked so brassie in red plaid.

Birdies, eagles, even stymied
golden ferrets hooted and hollered as winter's
blue sky carried a tiny white ball beyond infinity.

Santa scanned the valley yonder,
time to head North as the wondrous
January sunset faded over the aprons of emerald.

"Aprons! Oh niblick!" he muttered,
knowing the sequined Mrs. Claus waited dinner,
although she was resigned to the fact he lived fore green.

Donning a red apron sparkled
with snowflakes, hopeless, she knew her war on green
velvet was endless, so she just kissed his bald head when he arrived.

12/22/08
HO, HO, HO!!!

Shuttlecock Bed and Breakfast

Whoa, Nellie! echoes throughout the canyons as
we rode into the dawn stillness of a sleepy sheep
& ostrich dude ranch, a no frills bed & breakfast.

Prancing, the proud, freckled-fanny Arabian
mare wore her calico mane akin to a ruffle-like
cape draping over her shoulders like a poncho.

Detecting imaginary cheers, she struts onward,
her crimped strands wag and whip high creating dusty
puffs of feathers, her fleece-cloaked rider dismounts.

As sunup ganders, guests primp and preen, gathering
their offspring as a feast will begin as they flock to the
stockyard breakfast hall without a twitter or a peep.

Clutches of flapjacks nest on iron platters garbed with
churned butter and thick honey, kettle coffee, mutton bacon
and goose eggs, feathered bouquets style our tables.

3/11/09
Feathers

Silly Scab Conspiracy

Pick, pick, just pick
at the multi-colored, crusty scab
crookedly outlining my bony shin, I perch atop this hill.

Layer, layer by layer,
if peeled precisely, the most gorgeous beauty
mark will appear or I will ace my German classes.

Stretch, stretch, I stretch
every limb inhaling like a Yoga guru then scan
the valley below as Ich hauch die luft (I whiff the air).

Perfect, perfect, just perfect
is the absurd rhythm of lyrics sung by
the twittering, fluttering choir of Aspens.

Soothe, soothe, please soothe
my frazzled psyche, delusional,
I want to whip out my machete.

Chop, chop, vigorously chop
every stinkin' quaking tree down, ouch,
I cut my arm, oh goodie, another scab to pick.

3/4/08

Challenge:
(1) An example of false cause and effect logic
(2) Use a foreign language phrase
(3) Make a nonhuman object do something human
(4) Change direction or digress from the last thing you said

Sin of Silly Walks

To walk or not to walk the chalk.
Are you drunk on didactic form or high on free verse?
I trip and traipse down the triplet trail
another fairy tale comes to mind as a vision
of lurpy ostrich quills tickle me to the bone.

I idle, then sidle and stroll, assessing syllables,
I self-nessly saunter down sunny sonnet sidewalks,
a simple sashay here, a ridiculous roam there
my ludicrous limp makes me laugh
but this giddy gait, gads, how goddy!

Haiku, well bless you
as you walk with a wacky-tacky whimsical waddle,
I toddle making me dawdle as I shrewdly sniff the roses
but am poked by a thorn forcing me to
weave and wander...fonder, ponder, yonder.

Foolish flounce or a silly mutt strut,
my butt swaggers to the beat of different drummer
as all creative beings do, we swiftly stride and skirt
issues of rambling ridicule or promenading prestigious
though, always honoring the Ministry of Silly Walks.

2/10
Monty Python RULES or is just as uniquely crazy as the rest of us!

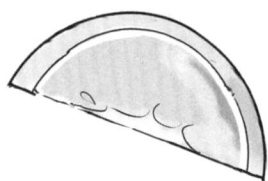

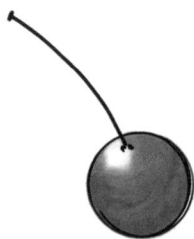

Snap!

Quivering, NO VACANCY was apparent
at the pre-snapped mousetrap,
my bouquet of holiday flowers seemed
so extravagant now, a little guy with
a jet black nose had nothing.

Snap!
One, too many times with a gnawing
attitude and opulence, this same little
guy skulked between our celebratory
footstep traffic selfishly scavenging,
pilfering yummy Christmas dinner crumbs.

Snap!
Fingers summon the inquisitively cautious
Doodle, now startled as purple polish
is applied to her toenails, she jerks away
backing into the Douglas Fir as
branches, abscissions flitter to the carpet.

Snap!
Grandpy breaks a candy cane
and dips it in a golden hot toddy
then grabbing a gifted jump rope,
he's transformed into the evening's
entertainment.

Snap!
My grandson then loops and snaps
an elastic-banded Santa hat over
Grandpy's head, steals his ice cream cone
and races out the door into the front
courtyard, magical winter mayhem explodes .

Snap!
Balancing this annual family affair
has me rocking in my Crocs
wishing to be lost in a similar-footed tub
with an unsalted vertiginous Margarita
being gulped before I Snap for good!

12/10/08
I snapped!

Sounds Like Candy

In New York on Long Island, old rusty burn barrels
stood stoically
in any backyard near the woods
awaiting the garbage that was piled up
next to them to be tossed
inside and incinerated.

To me and the neighbor girl, Gracie, the
stoically mounted
garbage was obviously sad and wanted
to play with someone,
so us two inquisitive 4-year-olds wandered over
and kicked a can.

Shiny and bright, the red and blue can
rested stoically
against a rock with what looked like
a red ball, a toy bubble on top,
Gracie kicked it again
and it rattled and rolled away from the pile.

Two fascinated little girls stared and
stoically pondered
what was inside to make it rattle, so I picked
it up and shook it,
wildly smiling
"Sounds like candy!" We giggled.

The funny bubble top, though baffled us for a time,
fiddling stoically
two 4-year-olds finally finagled a way
to pop it open and wow,
shiny, crystal, sparkly thingies
awaited our childish curiosity.

So what sounds like candy and looks
stoically like
candy, must in every sense
of anyone's playful world,
be the real thing, the forbidden treat,
treasures...candy!

Horrifically, the candy wasn't good
stoically screaming
we ran to our mommies as the pain
increased and burned,
our mouths, our tongues on fire
not knowing what happened.

Rushed to the hospital, all I remember is being
stoically rocked
by a humming nurse with a crisp white hat,
comforting me from the scary
daytime nightmare
of the never-to-be-forgotten DRANO adventure.

Circa 1962

4/18/15

The infamous burn barrel.

Soup and Sinkers

Chicken soup, carrots sweet,
we slurped, we ate, we laughed

laughed at the news, conversation
and Jeany's yucky pie donation, gift

gift of food for caucus house volunteers,
priceless, but butterscotch should be brownish-gold

gold, not dirt brown with lumps,
smooth brassy caramel in color

color of voters, the election was a
titanic issue like Jeany's biscuits

biscuits, tasty yet heavy like sinkers
grandpa used on his fishin' pole

pole dancing chitchat caused Michael's
eyes to grow big and round like the dots

dots on the Dominos we played
eating ice cream and giggling

giggling with wine and coffee, coddling
kittens who also dreamed of chicken.

11/5/08
Anadiplosis of an election evening with The Pontrellis

Spectacular Sky-bound Sorties

Flagged pylons, roaring
propelled pilots intercept
wind, earthlings beware!

9/3/09
Reno Air Races

Substitutionary Locomotion

Sleek fins with shiny scales
sparkle and twinkle, smoothing
as I slither off the rocky seaside, dipping
and diving into sapphire waves sashaying
with exhilaration, the exuberant evening tide augments.

Long luscious, golden
strands highlight my siren-red
tresses, my mane croons over my drenched
doeskin freckled shoulders reaching my scales, yet barely
shelters my perky bosom, I dogpaddle into Atlantis' briny depth.

My sexy, iridescent
imperial-purple lower half
seductively glistens, glows and glimmers;
I twist and turn innocently provoking flirts from sailors
triggering total distraction, hearing all too often, *man overboard.*

Dolphins spout and shout,
catfish whirl and twirl mocking the
seasick, hypnotized swabbies while bountiful
schools of submarine societies focus on their freestyle
from the Java Sea to the Persian Gulf and onto the Bay of Bengal.

I linger in my bizarre exotic,
aquatic wisdom, but a mysterious frequency
agitates the solace of my watery fairy dreamscape;
forcing the urge to stretch, to elongate my fin, to moan
as glitter and fireworks arouse me from a coma-like slumber.

My legs encapsulated,
cloistered by azure sheets, sequined blankets
and a miffed, multihued quartet cocoon of pelican-gray felines,
dreaming of cod and calamari; awakened by their fantasizing human
who thought she'd become a mythical mermaid—
in truth, she can't even swim.

10/22/08

Subtle Details of Ignorance

All around me
I see the fine print
black miniscule, unreadable words
secretive codes
in cloak-and-dagger fonts
mostly unreadable or indigestible
prompting anxiety within the would-be reader
a false sense of security whereas
you consent to the nature of a perplexed agreement
to acquire
operate
or borrow said item
from a for profit
not to be confused with a professional
yet distrusting company
whose skeptical jurisdiction dictates how to do that
but not to do this
specifically on a not-to-be-faulted
odd-numbered day
at precisely 5:13pm
tip-toeing uncomplicatedly into a sterile office
first left
then right
and flapping your arms like a gooney bird
during the likelihood of a three-quarter coyote moon
while Sierra sagebrush whistles computations
with westerly winds of negotiations
limiting themselves of any liability,
theft or vandalism
during your possession of said item
including exclusions and optional requirements
deemed necessary in concurrence
as long as you agree to give up your first born
sign on the dotted line
and not take the item into Mexico.

8/26/09
This rant is dedicated to the gibberish provided by
Rental Car Company Agreements

Suffocating Utterance

The fog plumed through the gunshot
holes in the train windows
like muddled family secrets intertwined
amid the essence of nightmare portals.

Grandma knitted the dream openings
closed so no one rescued us, perpetually
holding our life in her hands as if
to suffocate any chance of survival.

Weird love is to an open sky as loathing
is to cold, dark caverns of hellish delicacies
as family members dangle questions,
preaching disgust on past transgressions.

We giggle and snicker, nip on limes and sip
on wines knowing so well the past is past
then drunkenly drizzle honey on each other
and jump into Grandma's feather bed.

Up is like down when challenged with a
tour de force, a masterpiece of twisted
utterance in hopes of amusing toxic peers
who closely ponder with sincere absorption.

3/4/09
Wild Women Wickedly at Work.

Summer Delights Gone Bad

> Primed...
> farmers' market season
> begins and already abundant
> sweltering temps loiter
> scrutinizing sweaty hats that flop,
> earth-friendly canvas bags
> and muggy pups clutched
> by shoppers, strolling and tasting.

Spoiled...
moldy berries in green plastic
baskets are secretly ensconced
in crates behind the smiling farmer
while peaches and tomatoes tumble
off displays to their death while
their sweet juices simmer
on the littered sidewalks and asphalt.

> Radiated...
> summer heat permeates,
> the suffering produce rots
> as the day lags, but whipping
> winds refresh bargain hunters,
> though it disconcerts
> the temporary tent city, farmers
> hang on like Mary Poppins.

Fatigued...
the zealous crowd thins,
farmers sit a spell backhanding
the sweat from brows,
the rusty truck tailgate falls open,
empty crates are stacked in rows,
the ceramic statue salesman
sullen, sells nothing again.

> Scattered...
> wilted, silky corn husks
> and limp green beans
> await the clean-up crew
> whose job security is
> well secured by dog-flaunting,
> slap-happy, sloppy shoppers...and...
> Oh, crap, dog poop again!

3/2/09
Farmers' Market Management Rocks.

Sun-Dried, Baked or Broiled?

A forgotten day's blistering sun
overrules tattered thoughts,
a braided rope hammock
imprints my cradled body.

Perspiration drizzles down a
sun-baked chest like a summer's rain,
gentle breezes sneak by
taunting my heat-zapped body.

Eyelashes unlock, lids
raise slowly like a theater curtain
on opening night, blue irises
zero in on a crooked backdoor.

Pathetically, my limbs dangle
over the hammock's edge
uprighting myself causes my toes
to suffer the hot patio below.

100 degrees, the weatherman has won
today, fat chance for snow. The white
rope sling sways my sun-dried body
in rhythm with the vertigo, dizzy silence.

Like barbequed chicken, broiled
skin tingles. Twinges and throbs alert
a now pensive brain: go inside! Humans
are not designed to be well-done.

Tan, bronze, golden: totally, socially,
acceptable summer season colors.
Real cool. Real chic. Will reality
finally set in before the cancer does?

10/22/99

Sunrise, Sunset

Backlash of noodle heads
merge recklessly
causing mesmerized, propulsive power mongers
to hastily exchange excoriating gestures
while emotionless pumpkin-colored barriers
proudly protect the incarnation
of a neglected, concrete bowl,
sobriquet "Spaghetti!"

2004 - Intertwine words: Backlash, mongers, excoriating & sobriquet.
Gotta love our I-80 & Hwy 395 Construction Cluster

Sweet Smell of Success

A pungent bouquet of achievement
easily turns into stench and mystery
when one enthusiastic personality thrives whereas rivals
decay. As not all humans flourish
at the same velocity, safeguard your tangy, unspoiled
happiness as it can quickly begin to reek
from the musty aroma of jealousy. Euphoric
as you may feel,
a sourpuss or odiferous, ungrateful rat may lurk
waiting to inhale your jubilant breath
as if to commandeer the fragrant bliss.
But as an ever blossoming artist,
you triumph, no matter how much whiffing and sniffing
occurs, scoundrels will attempt to defeat
the pinnacle of success you
unknowingly or purposely flaunt. Amid the aftertaste of deception
and the lingering scent of envy, perhaps this
unworthy adversary's luck will change
as an excess tinge of your eagerness rubs off and they, too,
may experience the lasting effect of
Parfum de Prevail!

11/28/07

Tea Time

Each of our weekly tea gatherings
at Joyce's home began with choice:
leave your crap at the door or just leave,
choose a cup and tea bag from a limitless array,
which side of this charmed table would welcome you.

No matter the ebb and flow that may be
whooshing within your brain, Joyce gently
tunneled deep into her perceptual satchel of
wisdom for rejoinders and retorts gathered from experience
of eight decades in an earthsuit and an ethereal multiplicity past.

Tea time was a sincere relationship of
mystical banter such as seasonal debates,
corroboration of zeal, poetry, magic and muses,
and where we learn that giving up and coming out were
cathartic expressions of simplicity like baby quails and cottontails.

4/28/15
Joyce Cannon and our Wild Women on Poetry

The Cook is Goosed!

Spiked just right, the eggnog is ready for all to sip
with celery, carrots and chips to dip!

Football game cheers are heard from afar
preparing a meal solo, insane, so bizarre!

Luckily, White Zin's calling my name,
could be no dinner, now that's just a shame!

No one else in the kitchen, just me and the dog,
uncooked food sits, my head's in a fog!

No bird nor potatoes in the oven at this rate,
with looks of things dinner will be nil or just late!

I sit and I rock and I drink a bit more,
holiday dinners have become such a chore!

Gathering of laughs, recipes are collaborated,
but football games and parades keep me isolated!

Oh well, I can do this, no more of that moan,
it's back to my wine and my handy cell phone!

Snow disguises the driveway, winter I desire,
but today it's the cute pizza guy I most admire!

Thanksgiving 2006

The Dark Side

Walking the dark land beside you
step-by-step,
shadows serve as stoic constants...
we ponder your usage of muses
we savor your originality
we share victory or sadness
we stay close as you suffer pain or coddle fear.

Amplified laughter and prolific tears persuade
your paradigms to shift,
personal sandcastles emerge...
your growth, success and anxiety
mushroom in every direction,
the universe applauds, I cheer
with silent thunder, I am your dark side, your riptide.

10/17/10

The Day Before Winter's Rebound

Initiating nature's tennis match,
birds of every flock and feather ricochet back and forth
from fence boards to seed feeders
saluting seasonal resilience,
perched upon front porch steps, I join the excitement
realizing just the day before
I huddled in front of a roaring fireplace.

Nurturing afternoon warmth emanates,
nudging all things great
and small to emerge from winter blankets,
tiny young buds and broods uncoil from slothful hibernation,
each squinting at sunshine's first cloudless journey
despite the fact the day before
WELCOME mats were secreted under snow.

Appreciating every defrosted moment,
green and yellow grasshoppers play leapfrog,
paper-whimsy cocoons prepare to open and take flight,
and spiders venture into dry birdbaths,
while songsters rehearse on high wires,
bearing in mind the day before
leftover leaves were launched into orbit by an unruly squall.

Transitional days before spring are so crucial,
a sluggish human spirit begins to recoup
fleeting finances, regroup disregarded goals,
replenish stagnate souls allowing
cabin-craziness to subside
given that the day before
was once tomorrow and winter blues need to lie dormant for a spell.

3/9/10
The day before...

The Mentalist

Ten hungry fingers grip the metal handles of a pointed
sign spinning too fast, upside down, backwards,
nowhere, but waving everywhere.

Crooked eyes taste the inquisitiveness and mind-read
each gawking driver as they speed by
going somewhere, anywhere.

Whoosh of cars trigger blistering screams from the hot
asphalt forcing echoes of miserable
temperatures to bare legs.

High above, our solar glow scolds and scalds unhatted
heads while ecstasy booms from a stereo headset
prompting clumsy dance dis-coordination.

From soul to sole, Tourettes or caffeine creates bee-bop
rumbas and erratic gestures as unlaced sneakers
rearrange stubborn sidewalk cracks.

10/30/08
(Mind twist of sign waivers everywhere)

The Parent Trap

Our knight's shining armor
was actually a shiny silver
steamer trailer in the dusty
Dude Corral Trailer Park in Sparks, NV.

Train tracks, a stone's throw kept
our spike-heeled Mom chasing
after three little girls who now
have the sweetest, smelling Dad.

Three-piece suits in every color,
ties, shiny belt buckles,
cowboy hats, cowboy boots,
he was handsome, dreamy

Brown Derby beer and plain
bologna sandwiches, a favorite,
Army rations for Sunday dinner,
Bonanza and his kids.

Battle ships, aircraft carriers, fighter
jets constructed of paper and pencil
and plastic—playing make believe
when life was frantic and scary.

Big sis, Terry had a neighborhood bike repair
shop with Dad's tools, an unforgettable
turtle wax day. Furious but he loved her,
she got a Secret Sam set for Christmas.

The sound of a broken chair meant
no Sound of Music for Patty
and me, one of many spirited scuffles
for Dad to referee, but nurture.

He wiped our blood when we
got hurt, he wiped our noses
when we were sick, he wiped
my tears much too often.

I was his favorite because I
wanted to be—attentively, he
taught me to tell time, sternly
his finger tapped my collarbone.

Richard arrived casting smiles
and swinging casts, named
for Dad's mysterious friend whom
we'd never know or did we?

Tommy, another screamer in
a baby seat, we loved him but
forgot him on occasion under the
pile on the famous the coat chair.

Stubborn, huggable, international
man of mystery who could always
break the tension with his roaring
laughter or his Donald Duck impression.

Dad, I miss you and love
you for the time we had
together as the lead in our
very own Parent Trap.

Hope you get some acting work
up there, but please remember
you don't have to BS God,
just flash him that great smile.

11/14/02
To Dad—Love, Peg

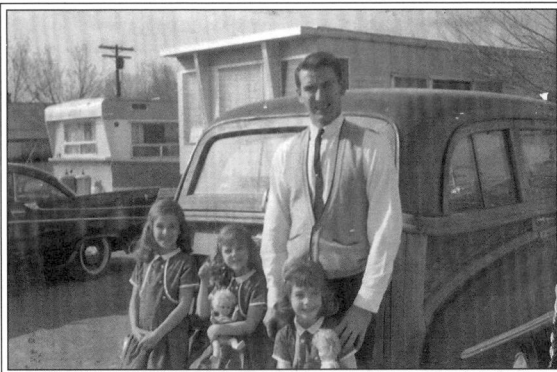

The River's Bitch Process

Swirling currents band together
pushing, pulling, shoving and begging,
thrusting audaciously forthwith and back,
a weakened Poplar is jammed, rammed
into a confident, chaotic abyss.

With orderly embrace, systematic disciplines
 encircle the helpless spirit
encouraging the eddies of reality,
once free, the stranded tree is besieged,
occupied by combat, meshed in crisis.

Foot-travelers cross the downtown bridge
matching each footstep with
the deafening crash of waters below,
the river chatters, splatters
across their wandering, unconcerned thoughts.

Consumed by Spokane's roar, passersby
and observers aren't fazed, instead
are intertwined in their own rush of existence
as tangled, mangled branches
collide against sturdy rapids and fierce boulders.

Forever jammed like moss on the north point of life,
the river owns scattered stragglers,
the streets own scattered souls
until one season for some reason, freedom
then escape occurs without warning.

4/28/10
My Spokane River Obsession

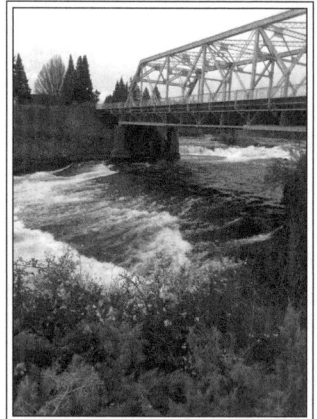

Til Death Do Us Part

More often than not
infatuation
attraction
lust
compels us
to promise our futures
to love and protect
in sickness and in health
for richer
for poorer. But having
to choose
breathing fresh air or
battling the constant waves
of second-hand smoke
to touch your beauty
to kiss your skin
to hear you laugh
to love you
only makes me pause
causing the
death of my passion
more often than not.

6/27/07

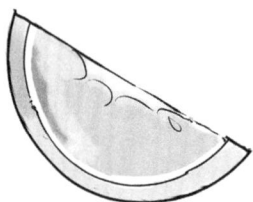

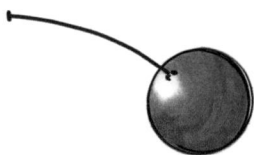

Tina, Christina,
How Does Your Garden Grow?

In her own little corner, in her own little world,
    she can be whatever she wants to be.
In her new house, a claw foot tub, or her rose garden,
    Any of these is where she's most HAPPY!

    She is Mom to J.J., Taz, William & Zen,
        to say the least, a manly foursome.
A good friend to many people,
    years past and those forth come.

    Though, doubtful, insecure and
        sometimes tearful at the drop of a hat.
Strong, independent, talented and caring
    is really where she is at!!

    So boldly she stages each room in her house
        with personalities, so unique.
Baseball or white rattan, Victorian or
    western, no, tied-dye for this week.

    Tina, Christina,
        how does your garden grow?
Many wonder yet admire your ambition
    and strength, we love to see you glow.

    Planted with love and sweat and muscle,
        Diet Pepsi and countless tears,
    Plant the thorns, puzzle down the green
        enjoy your paradise for years.

7/23/99

Tomato Sunrise

Once upon a time before the Black Rock Desert became the Black Rock Desert, a lush green, voluptuous paradise whispered through the mysterious valley.

Daisies danced in the northern Nevada breeze and summer corn stalks stood tall along the basin's 400 square mile border and Burning Bushes burned bright fire red during the summer/fall months.

As each season gradually approached, each plant gradually evolved. Individually, they took their turn as the natural transformation ritual occurred and the repetitive cycle went on for eons but then one winter, a peculiar feeling fell wide-spread across peaceful abyss.

As dawn began its ascent, all were cautious on this brisk March morn. Obvious change was occurring for those who existed in this wonderful paradise as brightness continued to rise in the eastern part of the flattened dreamland.

Winter was still in charge with the freezing of Smoke Creek, though amongst the crazy, cold weather-loving Daffodils, new foliage started to appear. Succulents like Sedum, Hens & Chicks, and Myrtle Spurge were popping up everywhere and graciously greeting their new neighbors. The new arrivals seemed friendly, but the elder plants were doubtful and then realized they were all drought-resistant and desert varieties. So why would they choose to grow here?

As spring sprung, Tiger Lilies welcomed the Sagebrush and Dusty Miller families. The community was growing with many new additions and by the onset of the summer months, the valley was enhanced with a grayish green palate. But then one day a strange mistral blustered through the nirvana.

The overwhelming zephyr was steady, unrelenting for days on end. Some of the original plant life began to dematerialize, vanished. The maize husks began to sway with the masterful wind and would eventually fall. They just couldn't stand up any longer. The Lilies became lethargic, the Sunflowers shriveled, the Mums collapsed, and the Forget-Me-Nots forgot what they were doing. In their places, sprouted Black-eyed Susans along with protruding Cacti and more dry gulch-tolerant.

But one proud old timer, the Beef Steak Tomato plants, held their ground—literally as tight as they could!

"We will not be intimidated or forced to leave our home – our ancestral roots run very deep here!" They proclaimed, "Change is good, but we will prevail with fruitful achievement!"

But as these plants watched their friends blow away, one by one, in the wicked, dry squall, they also witnessed in disbelief as many became sun-dried. The tomatoes huddled together to become as strong as possible! They agreed to "thin the herd"—to eliminate any vine members who weren't growing fast enough to be sustainable.

The sad elimination process was a must as the once plush Heirloom paradise made a quantum leap, an about face—the landscape changed completely! Amazingly but queer, it was still appeared to be a paradise, but of a different genre'!

Now as far as the eye could see was the flattest, smooth-as-silk sand playa. The expansive land had mutated into a prehistoric, hardpan lakebed where vegetation would never survive except at the base of the great Black Mountain at the north end of the valley where most of the tomatoes grew.

Less than flourishing at this point in time, there was only about a bushel-size garden of the Ragged Six and Brush Fire survivors. They knew perseverance was their only hope and prayed their plan would work. The plan was to climb with their vines up the mountain where there was some still precipitation—at least enough to sustain viability, but an uphill battle was inevitable and nearly impossible. By the end of the exhausting uphill trek, only one lone, but very large tomato succeeded in the quest for survival.

Wild Rose, as she appropriately penned herself, successfully made it to the top of the Black Rock summit. She surveyed the valley and knew she would endure life even if she was a lone warrior. At the crest, she strategically lodged herself between the two highest peaks, but after a fashion, became petrified.

Now every morning, Wild Rose, the last challenger of the Elimination Game, will forever greet the alkaline valley of the Black Rock Desert with her unique interpretation of "Tomato Sunrise."

3/3/05
Black Rock Poets challenge of an Ode to the Tomato Sunrise
upon the wall of Black Rock Pizza in Sparks, NV.

Tumultuous Upheaval of Wickedness

Morn, clear eastern sky
brisk smiles, cool Fall sunshine,
yellow streets honking.

    Oblivious jets
    harbor stoic death seekers,
    thunderous fire.

        Towers wheeze, grumble
        dreams, faith reduced to rubble,
        allegiance collapsed.

            Empathy unites
            brigades of buckets, man's best
            friend sniffs, digs, bares truth.

                Burning wretched pleas,
                panic accelerates, gray
                faces of ash sob.

                    City eclipsed, screams,
                    coworkers, tourists surface
                    horrified, blood, tears.

                        Besieged redeemers
                        stagger red, white and blue
                        pennants of passion.

                            Exhausted, shattered
                            hysterical disbelief,
                            white masks pray and mourn.

9/13/01

My poem was part of Western Nevada College's 2009 Always Lost project in Carson City and one of only five works on our 911 tragedy. It continues to travel today.

Uprising

Spring is springing with activity, voices echo in neighboring yards.
Rocks and boulders frame my backyard, my own border patrol guards.

A little shake here, a rattle there, Mother Nature kicks off a shudder.
Earthquakes, aftershocks vibrate, high wire birds hang on with a flutter.

Spring's last snow slowly melts, soaking the ground with nurturing goods.
Clear blue warmth sizzles undergrowth so tiny greens can grow as they should.

But the shakin' earthquakes trigger me to worry, wonder and wobble.
Is the big one just around the corner uprooting stones of cobble?

Rocks and boulders still line the garden's edge, a bit tilted, but at ease.
Raking and planting continues, spirits of the earth I will appease.

So the rocking and the rolling continue to growl, roar and rumble.
But spring commits to a course of action with quail and bees of bumble.

With recent rains, plants sprout though the soil, my garden is so sweet.
Tiny leaves flutter as birds fly from the eves, their nest echoes a tweet.

The seasonal intervals commence, uprisings are calm and collect.
Spring sets dreams and growth in motion, but keep gardens past in retrospect.

5/7/08

Urgency of Snowflakes

Capture on your tongue
cheap chill thrills, giggles linger
phenom melts, repeat.

12/7/10

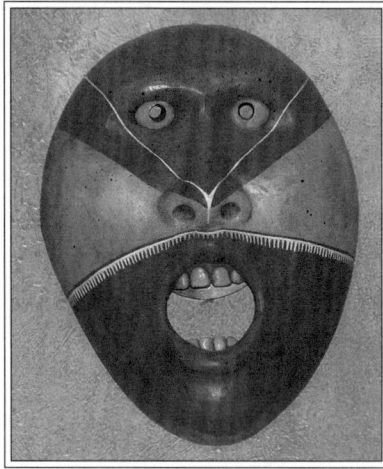

Velocity of Veracity

What is the attraction
of telling a little white lie? The urge
to tell a fib, to stretch the truth? At times, it may
be unavoidable, compulsory at best, yet candor
should be the wiser.

It is more important
to be human than it is to be important,
but humans feel the need to enhance the truth,
boost an inflated ego, embrace
a bogus smoke screen.

Like water as deep as forever,
honesty is a dazzling virtue that magnifies
sincerity, authenticity. We've all but forgotten what
accuracy is or some were never taught
to be reliable, loyal.

Frankly, our future depends
on truth, our village is faced with work aplenty
to fix bad guys, fight enemies and avoid unreliable
sources in hopes our true spirit discovers the wisdom to
dodge trickery and deceit.

7/16/09

Walking Backwards

Wisdom, infinite, retrospective or
Audacious, clouds of judgment cause us enabler and caretaker types to
Loiter in exhausting situations while our emotions are
Knitted into complicated apprehension. Mental commotion
Interlaces crisis and tension, wreaking havoc that may
Nullify the only chance at survival, a throbbing numbness burrows in, so I
Guard my heart, secure my spirit from theft, now an intense race.

Breathing new life into myself, I must
Act on a promise to resuscitate my soul before the warranty expires,
Calculating a cathartic cleansing, though all the way
Kicking and screaming, achieving the
Weaving out of tangled webs. Excited, yet
Armed, my backwardsness glimpses the lighted tunnel ahead, allowing me to
Recoil my fortitude and regenerate the essence within as I
Dawdle in the aroma of Blue Girl roses, then step forward, I
Sashay thru a rainbow of tulips to rekindle thyself.

1/6/10
An acrostic

Wandering Wonder

Longing to hear you breathe,
hold you close against me

Me and you currently exist
separated by tears, time and space

Space as wide as the gap in
the leer of toothless bums, homeless

Homeless, wandering lovers lost
in opposing emotional traffic jams

Jams, quandaries, difficult
interludes alienating passion, words

Words that strike out angrily
in need of recovery, in time

Time to again find each other,
to love again, someday

Someday, came and went
as did our longing.

4/1/01
Anadiplosis

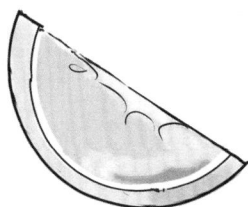

When I'm Gone

Geez, Laweeze!
What the hell?
Hey, L4 and L5, get off of me!
Yes, you jerks are pinching
the crap out of me!
Now our nerves are bitching
and spas-sm-ing
and oh shit, that hurts!
Yeah, go ahead—send
that good ole' referred pain
right down our left leg!
You are touching me?
Yes you, you bullies!
Every time either of you move,
you squeeze the nucleus guts out of me
and it will kill all of us soon!
I am trying to buck up,
trying to be brave, but
being a blown out disk
and leaking and irritating and just plain annoying
to all of my closest friends,
well, oh crap, now
I can't stop crying!
Well, I am sorry if
my oozing tears sting,
but I am out of control,
and you just wait, you'll
miss me when I'm gone!
You just wait, yeah, yeah,
you say you won't miss me now
but when they take me out and
put the new guy in,
there will be hell to pay!

Jesus Christ!
Ouch! Ouch!
God damn it, L4, lift up a bit, you bitch!
Thanks a lot, L5, I appreciate
you staying still
for at least a minute, duh!
Oh, don't you start, Sciatica Sister!
You, at least, get meds!
Oh, the rest of you, shut up!
You don't realize it, I mean it,
You'll miss me when I'm gone!

6/27/07
Ranting Ode to the L4-L5 Disk: 9/5/58 to 5/30/07

When Poets & Porn Stars Align

Progressive thinkers will command and control
the superficial world we recognize when poets and porn stars align.

A day of reckoning, of calculated conclusions,
the parallel of such vocations and professions, a resolve emerges.

The mirroring of intimates: trade secrets, whispers,
and expressions are appreciated, but only by genre-specific addicts or admirers.

Heroic couplets and heroic couples are revealed by disregarding
limits while solitary inner courses access the depths of the imagination.

Both artisans struggle equally with exhaustion,
mental practices tax the physical, isolated existence, a bridge of souls.

Groins of their minds birth anxiety for conversation and
miasma of guilt lurks, a sinister sky lulls each too much needed slumber.

In the blink of an eye, fatigue evaporates, free verse and free love
splendidly splice into epic, rhythmic proportion—vignettes and fishnets appear.

So no matter what professional modus operandi is chosen,
sensuous scenarios will be fleshed out when poets and porn stars align.

1/27/09

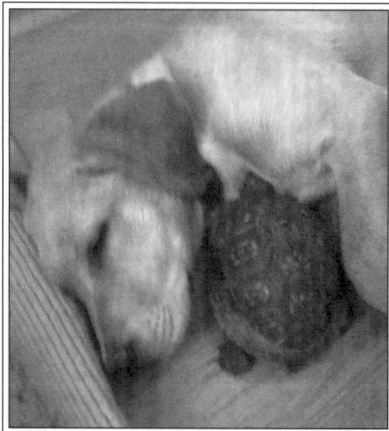

Challenge: Unite two completely different careers.

With Tense Precision of the Wrist, I Thee Aim

Blue gray eyes focus
arch of bone aligns arrow
my true love in sight.

2/18/09

Winter Blues on Cloudless Day

Although a peaceful distant skyline,
the canvas of robin's egg and azure
induce a twinge in my psyche
forcing my eyelids to 'batten down the hatches.'

Swiftly, yet artfully, the heavens let loose
littered, scattered, footloose phantoms
joined by voluptuous villainous veils of vapor
invading the vista with doom and gloom.

Spectacular nimbus billows of slate
and cinder stagger into view to tango
with the distorted remnant soldiers
of cobalt and battleship blue.

Pregnant thunderheads rumble
and tumble as soggy puffs
of nebulous nature sag overhead
resembling an overdue diaper.

The heavy-hearted squall robustly
molds and mutates while modifying
obscure, voracious poetry welcoming
cumulous overcast of cold sadness.

An angelic apparition appears daring
to appease and distract the darkened,
deceitful stranger, though soothing
salutations just aggravate tears.

Drizzling, discombobulated downpour
triggers despair forcing the overwhelmed
wooly nuisance to surrender as
eggshell-shaded shadows of cirrus satisfy.

Instantaneous unclouding commences,
merry murmurs and faraway echoes weaken
my weary winter blues with whispers,
"It's alright, Dorothy Dear, it was only a dream."

2004

Winter Wonderland Willingness

Taken for granted
all too often, our precious water
is not an unlimited resource
upon which all earthly beings
depend for
drinking, brushing, flushing, who
therefore, bank on the frigid, yet
willing intentions of winter
to produce a priceless gift,
no hidden agendas,
just the deliberate objective to
keep humans healthy with aspirations and inspiration,
grass green with hope and purpose,
wittingly motivated only by quality of life
for those who love voluntarily,
showering
all life forms with rain's romantic pour,
aiming for buoyancy while
the glacial goal of chilly days
garner fluffy clouds that
allow affectionate sunshine
its due, coddling and lulling
a garden to slumber, while
proliferating underground, though
prematurely, on occasion
encourage spirited, inquisitive
buds of optimism to pop up
through the freshly fallen
blanket of snow.

12/29/08
Intentions

Gratitude

Besides Dale Rew and Joyce Cannon, **big mushy thanks** goes to Kim Henrick, Jeany Pontrelli, Barbara Jean, Patty Cafferata, Vivian Olds, Kathleen Taylor and the late Shirley Howlett!

My writing cohorts in *Black Rock Poets, Wild Women on Poetry, Linebreakers' Revolution,* and *Mostly We Drink* pushed me in one direction or another; gave scarlet pen critiques; and contributed to the challenges from where many of these poems originated. I was also a drop-in at *Black & White Poets* and *Ash Canyon Poets.*

I truly loved being a groupie, but appreciate the isolation necessary to create something audacious!

I'm also thankful for my constant writing companions, my trusty sidekicks:

— *Flip Dictionary* by Barbara Ann Kipfer
— *The Nine Modern Day Muses (& a Bodyguard)* by Jill Badonsky.
— Joyce Cannon's CD, *Swords and Rainbows: A Sacred Portal to Growth and Healing*
— Blue October's *Foiled* album
— *Finding Neverland* soundtrack
— *The Awe-Manac* by Jill Badonsky
— *Medicine Cards* by Jamie Sands & David Carson

A few years ago, I asked a Swedish artist if she would be willing to draw a grapefruit with an attitude. She had never drawn a grapefruit...let alone one with a 'tude! But she did it and that grapefruit has patiently waited for the audacious moment to be the lead in her own production.

Thank you, Turi Everett, illustrator of all things *Petfolio,* for bringing Miss Thingish to life. Dale & I can't wait to visit Sweden, but always look forward to your Northern Nevada visits.

Thank you, Frank Ozaki and Hillary Velázquez at Double Click Design, for making this book possible as my dream team.

Thank you to our family at Abbott's Printing for capturing my vision in print.

Rew's Recommended
Reference/Research/Reading Roster

Flip Dictionary .... Barbara Ann Kipfer, Ph.D.

The Nine Modern Day Muses (& a Bodyguard) .... Jill Badonsky

Coincidence or Destiny and
Stroking the Creative Fires .... Phil Cousineau

Rhyming Dictionary .... Bessie Redfield

Naked, Drunk, & Writing .... Adari Lara

The Writer's Essential Tackle Box .... Lynn Price

The War of Art .... Steven Pressfield

The Light Inside the Dark .... John Tarrant

Pencil Dancing .... Mari Messer

What's In A Word? .... Webb Garrison

Word Painting .... Rebecca McClanahan

Wild Mind and
Writing Down The Bones .... Natalie Goldberg

Let the Crazy Child Write .... Clive Matson

The Midnight Decease .... Alice W. Flaherty

The Demon and The Angel .... Edward Hirsch

Bird by Bird .... Anne LaMott

Between Heaven & Earth .... Beinfield, L.Ac.
& Korngold, L.Ac., O.M.D.

Time Management for the Creative Person
and *Rock to Riches* .... Lee Silber

Index

179

Testimonials

Peggy's poetry speaks to my soul.
She has a unique way of capturing
pain,
childhood
and wonder
transforming complicated fodder
into a picture
that helps heal anyone
and brings me peace.
I love how she makes
her words come alive
and her ability to tell a story pulls readers in
making us feel as if we were a part of it!
She inspires me and
touches my heart with her profound work.

—Amy Lewis
Perceptive Healer/Lover of Life
Empowering and Inspiring Women
@ CranioWave, Reno, NV

...never galopp faster
than your guardian
angel...

Illustration by Turi Everett

I love them all and they so fully bespeak Peggy!
Wonderful poetic truthiness!
And what a beautiful dedication...from the heart.
How proud Joyce must be of you!

—Vivian Olds
Unpretentious Poet/Educator/Artist/Photog
@ Desert Light Arts, Wadsworth, NV